FAITH OF OUR FATHERS

VOLUME ONE

Jesus Christ

E. Glenn Hinson

A Consortium Book

To My Colleagues on the Faculty
of the Southern Baptist Theological Seminary

Table of Contents

Introduction

Religion is almost a universal phenomenon in human experience. If it is significantly absent from any society, it is absent from modern ones in which science and technology have become autonomous. Primitive societies tie all aspects of their culture together with their religion. Religion pervades agriculture, medicine, family life, leadership, hunting, fishing, play—everything. Perhaps this is confirmation of the Apostle Paul's often cited remark in Romans 1:19 that "Ever since the creation of the world his invisible nature, namely, his eternal power and deity, has been clearly perceived in the things that have been made." Or Augustine's that "man, this part of your creation, wishes to praise you. You arouse him to take joy in praising you, for you have made us for yourself, and our heart is restless until it rests in you." (*Confessions*, 1.1).

God, then, the devout would say, has not left himself without a witness. Religion is evidence of that. Still, both Paul and Augustine knew another side of this story. The other side is that humanity has not always perceived God well, whether in nature or elsewhere. Although human beings "knew God," to use Paul's words again, "they did not honor him as God or give thanks to him, but they became futile in their thinking and their senseless minds were darkened." They "exchanged the glory of the immortal God for images resembling mortal man or birds or animals or reptile" (Roman 1:21, 23). Put in modern context, they substituted service of machines as an end in itself, money, possessions, influence, power, activities, and lots of other things for God. They turned temporary things into ultimates.

The world religions, including Christianity, fit in here. All the world's religions have had prophets and reformers of some kind. Most believe that God has broken through the cultural wrappings and perversions in particular ways to get humanity back on the right track. They continually raise their voices against idolatry in its myriad forms, the substitution of proximates for ultimates.

Christianity is the product of a succession of prophets and reformers of religion. By its own interpretation it harks back to Abraham, who left the civilization of Mesopotamia to take up the life of a nomad in the near east. It continued through the prophet and reformer Moses and the prophets of the Old Testament. It reached its definitive form, however, in Jesus of Nazareth.

In this line God was breaking through with *particular* revelation of his will and purpose for humanity. He has spoken in nature. He has spoken in history. But nowhere has he spoken as he has spoken in these. Here his will became transparent in a way never achieved in human history. In Jesus of Nazareth it became all the more transparent. As the author of the Letter to the Hebrews put it, "In many and various ways God spoke of old to our fathers by the prophets: but in these last days he has spoken to us by a Son, whom he appointed the heir of all things, through whom he also created the world. He reflects the glory of God and bears the very stamp of his nature, upholding the universe by his word of power" (Hebrew 1:1-3). Or the author of the Gospel according to John: "And the Word became flesh and dwelt among us, full of grace and truth; we have beheld his glory, glory as of the only Son from the Father.... For the law was given through Moses; grace and truth came through Jesus Christ. No one has ever seen God; the only Son, who is in the bosom of the Father, he has made him known" (John 1:14, 17-18).

That, then, was the early Christian self-interpretation. God took the initiative to communicate himself so that, despite their natural tendency to distort his message, human beings could comprehend. A bold claim, indeed! "Pure fantasy!" some would exclaim. "Has it any basis in fact, in reality?"

The historian can give only a partial answer. Whether, in the final analysis, someone believes such a claim will depend on many factors—his predisposition to believe, cultural conditioning, family influences, the work of Christians, and many others. From one angle it does make sense, that is, from the point of view of communication of truth. The most accurate communication is that which is most direct and specific. Nature and historical events are not direct and specific modes of communication. Neither is the spoken word. The writer, for example, cannot be sure you are interpreting the words and ideas in this book the way he intends them to be heard. A myriad of factors will have conditioned you to respond with a certain understanding. If he could pour himself, ideas and all, into you, if he could become you, he could be much surer that you would understand accurately. For humans, despite some talk of neural transplants, metamorphoses of this type are at best remote possibilities. It is the Christian conviction, however, that God, in some mysterious way, poured himself into the life of Jesus of Nazareth in order to communicate himself, his purpose, without distortion. The mystery is that He did so without also relinquishing his ubiquity, his everywhereness. God's Word was incarnated in the life of Jesus.

How and why did Christians come to believe in incarnation? The answer to these questions is the answer to the origins of Christianity. As such, it is exceedingly complicated. It is complicated by the fact that while Christianity claimed not to be novel, there was something about this movement which distinctly separated it from its parent, Judaism. The distinctive factor was the belief that in Jesus of Nazareth, crucified and risen, God had inaugurated a new era in the history of salvation, indeed, in the history of humankind. The age of fulfillment, long dreamed of by the people of Israel, had dawned. God had not begun a new people, but he had arranged a new covenant. The new covenant, predicted by Jeremiah, based membership not on ethnic or national ties with Israel but on interior commitment. The possibility of membership was thus universalized in a way not considered possible under the old covenant. Israel under the new covenant was destined to incorporate Gentiles in a manner Israel under the old covenant never dreamed possible.

It was a reinterpretation of the covenant, therefore, which gave birth to Christianity as a distinct religious movement. The next question is: Where did this interpretation originate? Scholars have answered differently. During the highly critical era of the nineteenth century, the German history of religions school viewed Christianity as one of several oriental mystery cults which invaded the West in the same period. The founder of Christianity was not Jesus of Nazareth but Paul of Tarsus. Some scholars doubted even whether Jesus had ever really lived. Rather, they theorized, Paul invented him in order to give credibility to the dying and rising God myth of the mystery religions. Paul had no interest in Jesus' actual existence.

Subsequent research has shattered this theory completely. For one thing it has turned up references to Jesus in non-Christian sources, both Roman and Jewish, which prove beyond a shadow of a doubt that Jesus did live. For another it has demonstrated that Paul, although he may have had some knowledge of hellenistic mystery cults, derived most of his thought from his rabbinic background. He was certainly no devotee of a mystery religion. For another it has shown that, even after Paul, Christianity did not jump incautiously into the patterns of belief and practice of the competing mystery religions. If it accomodated, it accomodated externals rather than essentials. It used some of their language perhaps, but it did not borrow its basic beliefs. Indeed, nothing stands out more in early Christian writings than caution even in use of language. Finally, research has shown that the Old Testament exerted an immense impact in the shaping of Christian thought and life in the first several centuries.

In the last analysis it must have been Jesus of Nazareth who reinterpreted the covenant. To affirm that is not to deny that Paul played a premier role in the shaping of early Christianity. The Book of Acts and Paul's letters leave little doubt as to his importance. Without him, surely, Christianity might never have broken the bonds of Judaism and became a universal faith. But Paul saw himself not as the founder of a new sect of Judaism, much less as the founder of a mystery cult, but as a faithful interpreter of Jesus. He counted his Hebrew and Pharisaic background as so much refuse "because of the surpassing worth of knowing Christ Jesus my Lord" (Phil. 3:8). True, that meant knowing Christ as risen Lord. And Paul could say that, "even though we once regarded Christ from a human point of view, we regard him thus no longer" (2 Cor. 5:16). He did not mean by such a statement, however, that Jesus' actual historical existence had no significance for Christianity. The very words of Jesus had a normative significance for Paul. Accordingly, he distinguished his word from a word of the Lord on the matter of divorce. His word might be treated as advice or opinion, the Lord's could not (1 Cor. 7:10, 12)! It is hardly open to question that Paul meant by "the word of the Lord" words that Jesus uttered during his earthly ministry.

Jesus himself, then, is to be seen as "the founder of Christianity," as C. H. Dodd phrased his role. This would not mean that he founded Christianity in the shape it now bears nor even in the shape it bore in A. D. 100. Obviously many persons, in addition to Paul, contributed to its shaping over many centuries. Actually Christians would say that Jesus as risen Lord has been working through all of these person through the centuries to shape his Church. The process is unending. Nevertheless, Jesus in the flesh *began* the process. He founded Christianity in the sense that he announced the dawning of the age of fulfillment of Jewish hopes in and through his own person and ministry. What Israel's prophets had pointed to, he proclaimed and bore witness of in his person and ministry. His calling of disciples, his proclamation, his parables, his "mighty works," his activities which eventually led to his death—all announced the inbreaking of the Kingdom of God.

What happened in Jesus' brief ministry, however, is not adequate to explain by itself the development of early Christianity. In the nineteenth century, as a matter of fact, it was a truism of liberal Protestant theology that "Jesus founded no Church." Rigorous critical study was used to sustain this view. The fact is, in the two instances (Matt. 16:18, 18:17) in which Jesus used the Greek word *ekklesia*, he doubtless had in mind the assembly of Israel and not a Church composed of his followers. The Church, therefore, has to be seen as an outgrowth of his teaching and activities and, ultimately, of an overwhelming conviction among his followers that, though crucified, he had risen. The resurrection of Jesus, seen as a divine seal of approval on his life and death, is Christianity's source of origin.

Had the followers of Jesus believed that he remained in the grave, whatever he had taught them about himself, the movement would have died quickly. Movements with promising beginnings have petered out. Here was a movement with a most unpromising beginning, its founder crucified as a criminal in a far flung corner of the vast Roman Empire. It took a powerful incentive to pump life into such a movement, so that within a century it would plant conventicles in every part of the Empire and as far east as Mesopotamia and within three centuries become the acknowledged religion of the Empire which once persecuted its adherents.

By themselves Jesus' teaching and career would fail to provide such incentive. Only the unshakeable conviction that he had triumphed over death supplied it.

Now a historian, as historian, can neither substantiate nor deny the resurrection of Jesus as an historical event. The evidence of witnesses for it is as strong or stronger than the evidence needed to confirm most historical happenings. It includes not only secondary but also primary, "eyewitness," testimonies. In two respects, however, this event differs from other historical events and thus cannot be substantiated as are the latter. First, it is *unique*. Various ancient documents bear witness to resuscitations. These, however, fall into another category than the resurrection of Jesus, for they represented momentary restorations of vital functions. Those so raised would die again in the normal way. The resurrection of Jesus, therefore, belongs in a category of its own. It has no parallel. As a unique event, secondly, it is trans-historical. Something historical did happen, to be sure. The empty tomb evidence indicates that the corpse of Jesus disappeared.

Critics of the story had to invent explanations for this *fact*. But something also happened which lies beyond the realm of historical investigation. Jesus *reappeared* to some of his followers. He reappeared in such a way that they could "see" him with the eyes of faith when others could not "see" him.

Because the resurrection of Jesus is trans-historical, Christianity, in its confessions, has always inserted this as an essential article of faith. The Christian "believes the resurrection." He confesses his belief not as a historian but as a person. He cannot *prove* his faith.

What the historian can substantiate by the application of his discipline is *the impact which this belief had upon Christian origins and development*. The conviction pervades all early documents about Jesus. Indeed, scholars are more or less unanimous in the judgment that the evangelists wrote not "lives" of Jesus but "testimonies" to him which present him from the vantage point of the resurrection. The nineteenth century produced a number of "lives" of Jesus, some running into thousands of pages. The development of critical studies, however, showed the biographical enterprise to be nothing but a house of cards. Albert Schweitzer, in *The Quest of the Historical Jesus*, pointed up the fallacy of the whole endeavor. After the publication of his work scholars directed their energies toward examination of the *kerygma*, the Church's proclamation about Jesus. Studies of the *kerygma* reached a peak in Rudolf Bultmann's confident assertion that Jesus should be treated as a presupposition for Christian theology and history, not as part of either. Although some of Bultmann's students have raised the issue of a new "quest" of the historical Jesus, none has turned the clock back to the biographical stage. What can be known about him is, at best, his self-understanding.

Faith in Jesus as crucified and risen Lord, therefore, colored what early Christians wrote about Jesus' life and ministry. What this signifies is that no historian will claim to describe "what actually happened," as the German historian Leopold von Ranke thought he could do. He cannot have such confidence about writing the story of any event. Whatever uncertainties he may have about Jesus' life, death, and resurrection, however, he cannot doubt the impact belief in his resurrection had on his early followers, including the way they told the story. This conviction alone makes sense of Christianity's thrust into the Roman Empire and beyond despite its unpromising beginnings. But the conviction does not stand alone. It is inseparably tied to a conviction that God has disclosed himself in a whole series of events. These events reached a climax in Jesus. Out of them emerged the Christian Church.

To understand Jesus and the beginnings of Christianity, therefore, requires a study of this series of events. In the Christian view Jesus stood at the mid-point of the history of salvation. He came "in the fulness of time" (Gal. 4:4). The way for his coming was prepared both by the experience of Israel and the experience of Greece. These two experiences merged at a crucial historical juncture. They served, as it were, as pedagogues to Christ. They tilled a field which Christian missionaries planted. The crop prospered.

PART ONE

Waiting for the Messiah

1

A Covenant People

There were two tutors to Christ, Clement of Alexandria believed, one Judaism and the other Hellenism. Some Christians would contest whether he was right about the second, but none would debate the first. Jesus was a Jew, an heir of almost two millenia of the history of his people.

Precisely in what way the Jewish nation and religious faith came into existence is a matter of extensive scholarly debate. According to the Genesis account, they originated with Abraham, a nomadic leader of Haran in northern Mesopotamia, and his descendents. Many things in the Genesis narratives harmonize with information scholars have unearthed about the customs and events of the ancient east during the early second millenium B. C., but they do not allow a precise reconstruction of the story of the patriarchs. The most definite information concerns their entry into Egypt, perhaps along with the Hyksos invasion, around 1750 B. C., an event which provided the setting for the begetting of the monotheistic covenant faith of Israel.

The crucial event was the Exodus from Egypt, probably around 1250 B. C., and the crucial figure was Moses. The Exodus, from an early date, stood at the center of Israel's confession of faith (Ex. 15:1-18; Deut. 6:20-25; 26:5-10; Josh. 24:2-13). The covenant faith based upon the Exodus deliverance came into focus during the wilderness wanderings of

Israel. To what extent, even yet, it represented a genuinely monotheistic faith is a moot point. There is no doubt that Yahweh was *Israel's* only God. Was he the only God of all nations? Much later evidence in the Old Testament indicates that, whatever the theoretical answer to the question, the Jewish people frequently lapsed from belief in as well as service of Yahweh. They did not deny the existence of other deities; they simply claimed greater strength for Yahweh. Often, too, they lapsed into idolatry, the service of many gods in the land where they lived. If they were monotheists, they did not show it.

Whatever may have been the actual strength of Israel's monotheism, the concept of a covenant with Yahweh laid the foundation for monotheism. Moreover, influences of surrounding cultures notwithstanding, the covenant idea was unique. The origin of it was the Exodus experience. According to the account of Exodus 19, God acted out of mercy or grace, *hesed*, to snatch Israel from the claws of the Egyptians. On account of this mercy he elected a people, an unworthy one at that, a slave people. He turned back the Egyptians and bore them "on eagles' wings" and brought them to himself (Exod. 19:4). This is not the typical religious experience of a people frantically searching for God and finding him. It is the reverse of that. God sought and found a people.

What was involved in the covenant? For one thing, it put Israel in a privileged position with reference to Yahweh. The terms of the covenant read that "if you will obey my voice and keep my covenant, you shall be my own possession among all peoples; for all the earth is mine, . . . " (Exod. 19:5). Such a statement could be interpreted in a very bigoted manner, as it often was throughout Israel's history. If monotheistic, as the clause "for all the earth is mine" implies, it could become nationalist and racist. Such an interpretation doubtless lay behind the conquest of Canaan and the formation of Israel as a nation. Behind Joshua rather than Moses Israel proceeded to accomplish that gory task with a clear conviction that God willed it. He had promised Moses and their forefathers that they would "inherit" the land of Canaan. He would give it to them in battle. The only proviso was that Joshua and his people "do according to all the law which Moses my servant commanded you" (Josh. 1:7).

A broader interpretation broke through only on occasion, where the monotheism implied in the covenant became universalistic. Israel's experiences of defeat and captivity perhaps helped to hammer such an interpretation into shape. Scholars now debate how universalistic the author of Isaiah 40-55 was, but he could identify Cyrus, the Medo-Persian conqueror, as the chosen instrument of Yahweh (Isa. 41). Furthermore, he emphasized the universal mission of Israel, the "Servant of the Lord." In one "Servant poem" Yahweh declared, "It is too light a thing that you should be my servant to raise up the tribes of Jacob and to restore the preserved of Israel; I will give you as a light to the nations, that my salvation may reach the end of the earth" (Isa. 49:6). Malachi, almost certainly speaking in the post-exilic period, sounded an even more universalistic note: "For from the rising of the sun to its setting my name is great among the nations, and in every place incense is offered to my name, and a pure offering; for my name is great among the nations, says the Lord of hosts" (Mal. 1:11).

It was not until Jesus, however, that genuine universalistic monotheism came into its own. Even Deutero-Isaiah and Malachi let a kind of vindictive nationalism override their monotheism. At the opposite extreme stood prophets like Obadiah with his "hymn of hate," the scribe Ezra, who sought to establish Israel's identity around study of the Law in order to preserve it from assimilation by surrounding peoples, the Maccabbees, who tolerated no compromise to Hellenism, and the Dead Sea Covenanters, who would "love" the fellow covenanter but "hate" the "stranger". How the covenant with Yahweh should be interpreted was a central issue in the origins of Christianity.

Seen from one side, then, the covenant involved privilege.
From the other side, however, it involved obligation. Yahweh elected Israel not merely to bestow blessings but to render service. Israel was to be "a kingdom of priests and a
holy nation" (Exod. 19:6). Both phrases are pregnant with
meaning for the self-understanding of Christianity as well as
that of ancient Israel.

"A kingdom of priests" implies that Israel was more than a
political society. It was a nation with a religious purpose.
Deutero-Isaiah interpreted the religious purpose as to be "a
light to the nations" (Isa. 49:6). And in the post-exilic period
Israel did develop an aggressive missionary program, scattered as its people were in the Diaspora. Jesus himself attested
the intensity of this missionary impulse in his day when he
remonstrated with the scribes and Pharisees for traversing
"sea and land to make a single proselyte" (Matt. 23:15).

Before the Exile, however, Israel seems not to have grasped
the broader implications of this phrase. First came the conquest, which was not completed until the time of David (ca.
1000-961 B. C.). If any religious concern for other peoples
were involved, it meant their subjugation or their extirpation
in the name of Yahweh. The conquest, it is true, was seen as a
"holy war." But it was a holy war with one aim: to put Israel
in control of the "promised land." It was a test of strength
between Yahweh and the gods of Canaan. Yahweh was a
jealous God who would tolerate no competitors.

In the period of the monarchy, united under David and
Solomon and then divided under their successors, Israel left
little evidence of concern to represent Yahweh to the nations.
David busied himself with the completion of the conquest.
Solomon consolidated the administrative power of the
kingdom. In the process he sought to give an international
character to Israel, establishing ties with major powers,
developing manufacture, and strengthening his army with
modern implements. His most significant religious act was
the building of the Temple. This act, however, could be seen

as a narrowing of monotheism, for it implied God "dwells in temples made with hands." In his own religious outlook Solomon evidently moved in the direction of syncretism as his numerous wives brought with them the gods of other peoples. Solomon's successors in both north and south preoccupied themselves subsequently with the survival of their kingdoms. Both kingdoms, if we believe the prophets, barely retained their identity as Yahweh's people.

The fall of these two kingdoms, Israel in 722 B. C. and Judah in 589, and the deportation of the Jewish people to Assyria and Babylonia set the stage for Israel to become truly "a kingdom of priests." The people, led by prophets such as Isaiah, Jeremiah, and Ezekiel, doubtless discovered that God was ubiquitous. The fall of the Temple freed many of the territorial concepts of Yahweh. Most remarkable witness of this was a Jewish military colony at Elephantine on the river Nile. Founded about 587 B. C. evidently, this colony erected a temple in which they pursued a kind of syncretistic worship. Jews outside of Palestine, especially in Egypt, accomodated their faith to the surrounding culture. The result was the attraction of a significant number of proselytes and "god-fearers" to Jewish monotheism. Judaism tilled and planted well throughout the ancient world.

It is not difficult to see why Israel compiled a spotty record in fulfilling its priestly role. For most of its history the motley tribes which became Israel struggled to become and then to survive as a nation with a distinct religious identity and purpose. At some junctures territory and temple may have provided the most feasible means for establishing this identity. At other times fervent nationalism and study of the Law as the revealed will of God may have done so.

This concern for identity is reflected in the other clause which depicts Israel's covenant obligations, "a holy nation." The Hebrew word for "holy," *kadosh*, meant "set apart." Animals were "set apart" for sacrifice in the sense that they were being dedicated or consecrated to an explicit religious purpose. Israel's "holiness" as a people derived from the fact that they were "set apart", consecrated, to the service of a holy God. God was holy; his people were to be holy.

Both the moral and the ritual law of Judaism turned on this axle. The levitical law, in particular, stressed the *distinctness* of the Jew in his customs and undergirded it with a call to imitate God's holiness. Leviticus 11:41-45, for example, forbade eating things that swarm, "For I am the Lord your God; consecrate yourselves therefore, and be holy, for I am holy." The way of the covenant was a way of separation.

Maintenance of Israel's separateness was problematic throughout its history. In the period of the settlement in Palestine the tribes scattered throughout the land easily confused their beliefs and customs with those of peoples already living there. During the monarchy, foreign alliances led to the importation of foreign ideas and practices, including religious ones. Religious reformers and prophets had to remain vigilant against the incursion of Canaanite religion. Thus, for example, Elijah entered the lists against Jezebel, wife of Ahab, whose name itself suggests a connection with the cult of Baal. Elijah's theme was that Yahweh will brook no competitors. He is a jealous God, whose covenant demands complete and unquestioning commitment to him alone (cf. 1 Kings 19:10, 14).

Elijah's successors blamed Israel's failures and eventual defeat upon unfaithfulness to the covenant. If Israel and Judah would repent and commit themselves anew to the covenant, they insisted, God would save them. Some monarchs acted on these words and implemented reforms. In Israel, the northern kingdom, Jehu undertook a partial reform after his victory over the sons of Ahab (842 B. C.) wiping out Baal worship (2 Kings 10:28). But he evidently failed to purge some other forms of idolatry (2 Kings 10:29-31). In Judah, the southern kingdom, Joash (837-800 B. C.) also inaugurated a partial reform (2 Kings 6:1-3). The rest of the story of the monarchy was one of the ups and downs until the thoroughgoing reform of Josiah in Judah (640-609 B. C.), a century after the fall of the northern kingdom. It was during this reform that "the book of the law of the Lord given through Moses" was discovered in the Temple (2 Chron. 34:14). This discovery, almost certainly the book of Deuteronomy, restored the Mosaic covenant to the center of Israel's faith and life. Deuteronomy came down hard on Israel's absolute separateness. The invaders were instructed to kill all persons — men, women, and children — and even animals in cities they captured as their own "that they may not teach you to do according to all their abominable practices which they have done in the service of their gods, and so sin against the Lord your God" (Deut. 20:18).

If such reforms might have saved Israel and Judah at one stage in their history, they came too late. The Exile which followed (589-520 B. C.) created new challenges to Israel's holiness. The Temple was destroyed. When at last Cyrus enabled some to return to their homeland, Ezra and Nehemiah sought to consolidate the small remnant, few of whom represented the old governing classes, around restoration of the Temple and study of the Law. Because the people of the land intervened, fearing that restoration would lead to aggression (Ez. 4:1 ff.), the reconstruction of the Temple proceeded slowly with much prodding from Nehemiah. By this time the Law had become the focus of Israel's life, and it remained so from that time forth (about 450 B. C. on). Ezra inaugurated the scribal tradition which separated Jews and Jewish customs sharply from those of surrounding peoples. Mixed marriages were vigorously proscribed. Israel was "set apart" from the peoples of the land.

So long as the Persians ruled Palestine, the Jewish people encountered no severe obstacles or challenges to this policy of isolation. Although there is scanty first-hand information about Israel itself, it is well known that the Persians encouraged local rule and tolerated independent customs. The

Greek conquest of Palestine in 332 B. C., however, was to change that, for it was of the nature of Hellenism to impose Greek culture everywhere as the ultimate and superior culture. The covenant, seen in terms of "a holy people," faced its most serious challenge since the invasion and settlement of Palestine. The challenge became particularly strong in the second century B. C. as the Seleucids, Alexander the Great's successors in the East, pursued a deliberate policy of hellenization, forcibly imposing Greek customs, and claimed divine honors.

A crisis occurred when Antiochus Epiphanes (175-163 B. C.) sought to unify a fading domain against the threat of Rome in the West and the Ptolemies in the East. In line with this aim he zealously fostered worship of Zeus, calling himself the visible manifestation of Zeus, and sought to impose other Greek customs on his subjects. Meantime, some of the Jewish priestly aristocracy, seeking Antiochus' favor in order to gain political advantage, fell in with the scheme of hellenization. A certain Joshua or Jason (the Greek name) offered Antiochus a large sum of money and promised full cooperation with the royal policy in return for Antiochus' aid in obtaining the high-priestly office. He then proceeded to seize the office and set about actively to hellenize the Jews. He established a gymnasium in Jerusalem where Jewish youth, even young priests, participated in athletics, according to Greek custom, in the nude, shaved, wore Greek garb, and evidently even gave token recognition to the Greek gods Heracles and Hermes, who were regarded as protectors of the games. The whole affair shocked and offended conservative Jewish sensibilities no end.

Jason was outbid for the office by Menelaus, who may not have been of priestly lineage. To obtain money for his bribe of Antiochus, Menelaus stole vessels from the Temple and sold them. Then, in 169 B. C., he allowed Antiochus himself to plunder the Temple, removing its furnishings and even stripping the gold leaf from its facade (1 Macc. 1:17-24,

2 Macc. 5:15-21). This sacrilege enabled Jason to rally an army to unseat Menelaus. Faced with this open rebellion, Antiochus retaliated. In 167 B. C. he dispatched a large force under the leadership of Apollonius, commander of Antiochus' Mysian mercenaries. Apollonius massacred hundreds of Jews and enslaved others, looted the city of Jerusalem and pulled down its walls, and erected a citadel called the Aira to station his troops. The Temple ceased to be the property of the Jewish people and became a shrine devoted to Zeus and to the cult of Antiochus Epiphanes himself.

In December of 167 B. C. an altar to Zeus was set up in the Temple and swine's flesh offered upon it, the "abomination of desolation" referred to by Daniel (9:27; 11:31; 12:11; 1 Macc. 1:54).

The response of pious Jews was resistance to the death led by a group known as the Hasidim, from whom both Pharisees and Essenes probably descended. The Hasidim emphasized faithfulness to the Law. In 165 B. C. their resistance led to open rebellion under the leadership of a priest of the village of Modein, named Mattathias, and his five sons. The chief leader was Judas, called Maccabeus, "the Hammerer," whose nickname was given the revolt. Because Antiochus was entangled in a campaign against the Parthians, the Maccabean Revolt proved successful, and in December 164 the faithful rededicated the Temple. Ever since, the Jews have celebrated the Feast of Dedication (Hanukkah) in commemoration of this event.

The crucial events of this period assured the triumph of the Law in the religion of Israel. The faithful had courageously maintained the regulations of the Law in the face of torture and death at the hands of hellenizers. The canon of scriptures was being defined more precisely. By 400 B. C., the Pentateuch was canonized. By 250 B. C. the prophetic writings stood firm. Others were to receive gradual approval until finally the canon was closed at the end of the first century A. D.

Although the Temple and its Worship still held an important place in Jewish life, alongside the Temple, perhaps in the exilic period, appeared the synagogue. Synagogue worship focused upon instruction in the Law by scribes, experts in interpretation. As the Law increased in importance, so too did the interpreters of the Law and their interpretations. A set of rules for interpretation were devised. Traditional interpretations were handed down orally from great teachers until codified in the third century A. D. as the Mishnah.

Zeal for the Law was accompanied by the development of practical concern for conduct reflected in the so-called wisdom literature (Job, Proverbs, Ecclesiastes, Tobit, Ecclesiasticus, the Wisdom of Jesus Ben Sirach, and the Wisdom of Solomon). Wisdom originated early, perhaps in the tenth century B. C., but it was adapted in this time to describe the good life *under the law*. The essence of wisdom was to fear God and keep his commandments. He is blessed who delights in the law of the Lord and meditates on it day and night (Ps. 1:2). The Law regulated all aspects of life. It enjoined righteous behavior, honor to parents, sobriety, chastity, moderation, almsgiving, forgiveness, and religion of the heart. What it required was not an external but an internal obedience to God.

The Law was absolutized. In elevating it to a normative position the Mosaic covenant itself was deemphasized. The faith and life of Israel were thus detached to a degree from their historical moorings. Yet such a development was perhaps inevitable as the Jewish people sought to be "a holy nation." Historical circumstances often force people to shift their foundations. In the long run it was attachment to the Law which helped Israel to survive successive blows which could have obliterated their identity. Still, a problem arose when narrow legalism prohibited the discharging of the other aspect of the covenant, that is, as "a kingdom of priests." Here is where Christianity resisted and broke free both of Temple and of Law.

2

Jesus' Homeland and People

Jesus was born in an impotent and impoverished land. His homeland was the battleground of the great powers of the ancient world not because of its power and wealth but because it was the strategic crossroads of the near east. First one and then another of the giants controlled the crossroads and used it as a buffer against others. It was the chess board, its people the pawns of giants. Except for the brief stretch of history during David's and Solomon's reigns, these people had little to say about their own fate. Security for them depended, they frequently discovered, not upon their might but upon Yahweh, their God.

Some historians have used Israel as the example par excellence of the "spiritual theory" of history. According to this theory, Israel developed spiritually because she was deprived geographically and economically. She could not rely on fertile valleys like the Nile or Tigris and Euphrates. Quite the contrary; she became a nation in the wilderness wanderings, wherein survival hinged on divine inspiration much more than on material substance and power. Then, her "promised land" turned out to be less a land "flowing with milk and honey" than a land of uncertainty and want. To be sure, Palestine had some productive places, for example, Galilee. Here were produced grains, olives, fruits of various kinds, sheep, cattle, and other foodstuffs. But, on the whole,

13

Palestine was a land of the poor. Rainfall was meager, better along the coast than inland. Much of the soil was barren and rocky. Famines were common.

The yoke of oppression and poverty often weighed heavily upon the people of Israel. A tiny nation, however, could not easily throw off another nation's yoke. If the yoke was to be lifted, the big powers had to assist. Thus the Persians lifted the Babylonian yoke in 520 B. C. But then came subservience to the Greeks — first Alexander of Macedon, then the Ptolemies and Seleucids. Briefly the Maccabees managed to wrest freedom from the Seleucids and to set up a Jewish state. In 63 B. C., however, the Romans intervened and imposed their lenient but powerful rule.

The Roman yoke chafed the Jews more than any other, despite Roman leniency. Soon after Pompey's victory, the Romans snatched the scepter from the Hasmonean priests. They divided Jewish territory into five districts. In 47 B. C. Hyrcanus II, a Hasmonean, and Antipater, an Idumean, gained the favor of Julius Caesar by supporting him in his war in Egypt. Hyrcanus was rewarded with appointment as high priest and Antipater with Roman citizenship and the government of Judaea. Antipater appointed his sons Herod and Phasael prefects of Galilee and Judaea respectively. In 41 B. C. Augustus and Mark Anthony appointed them tetrarchs of the Jewish state. After a brief seizure of power as king and high priest by the Hasmonean prince Antigonus (40-37 B. C.) Herod the Great recaptured all of Palestine. The Romans recognized him as an "allied King" free from tribute but subservient to Rome in foreign relations, especially war, for which he had to supply troops.

Herod was an able person, but his entire reign (37-4 B. C.) was stormy. He faced opposition from the aristocracy, the Hasmoneans, Cleopatra of Egypt, and the Jewish people. Despite attempts to curry popular favor by remitting taxes in lean years, importing grain, and rebuilding the temple, he earned increasing enmity. The Jews despised him as a foreigner, as a liege of the Romans, and as a cruel murderer of his own family. His finest achievement, in many respects, was the furthering of the plans of Augustus in building, literature, and rhetoric.

Herod's sons scarcely did better than he. Archelaus, who ruled Judaea from 4 B. C. to A. D. 6, was the least liked. With his exile to Vienne in Gaul in A. D. 6 Judaea became a Roman province. Antipas, whom Jesus labeled "the fox" (Luke 13:32), ruled the tetrarchy of Galilee and Perea more wisely (4 B. C. - A. D. 39). Philip, tetrarch of Iturea and Trachonitis (4 B. C. - A. D. 34), was liked by his subjects because of his justice and benevolence in a Jewish minority area. At Philip's death his tetrarchy was incorporated into the Roman province of Syria, but it was granted in A. D. 37 to Agrippa I by the Emperor Caligula, along with the title of King. Agrippa (37-44) was popular with patriotic Jews because he was an heir of the Hasmoneans and with the Pharisees because of his concern for the observance of the Law.

The Roman procurators, who ruled Judaea, Samaria, and Idumea after A. D. 6, failed to reconcile the Jewish people to Roman rule. The Jews revolted when the new perfect of Syria took a census for the purpose of taxing Judea in A. D. 6. Numerous other revolts occurred, but all were quelled forcefully. Pilate, who governed from A. D. 26 to 36, was particularly unpopular. The Jewish antipathy grew until rebels mounted an all out effort to rid themselves of the Roman tyranny.

Fighting erupted in the reign of Gessius Florus. This unsympathetic procurator, according to Josephus, plundered entire towns and allowed robbers full freedom of action if they paid the proper bribe. Jewish patience was exhausted when he took seventeen talents of gold from the Temple treasury. The Jews repaid him by raising a collection for the "indigent" Florus. He took bloody vengeance for the insult. Eleazar, the high priest, signaled open rebellion against Rome by stopping sacrifices in behalf of Nero. Rebels captured the

Roman garrison at Masada and annihilated its troops. The war was on.

Widespread riots occurred among the Jews. In October of A. D. 66 they routed the legate of Syria, Cestius Gallus, when he tried to besiege Jerusalem. This victory united all Jewish people against Rome. Victory proved shortlived, however. In A. D. 67 Vespasian captured Galilee with a contingent of 60,000 troops. A year later he took Perea, western Judea, and Idumea. Nero's death in A. D. 68 interrupted his operations for a year. In July of 69 the Roman troops in Egypt and the Near East acclaimed him Emperor. Legions on the Rhine acclaimed Vitellius, but the latter was murdered in December. This opened the way for Vespasian to return to Rome in the summer of 70. His son Titus completed the victory, capturing Jerusalem in August, A. D. 70, after a seige of five months, and destroying the Temple and its inhabitants. A few guerillas held out for a time. The fortress at Masada fell last, in April, A. D. 73. Rome still ruled.

A later rebellion, A. D. 132-135, led by a certain "Simon, Prince of Israel," or Bar Kochba, fared no better. This revolt resulted from Hadrian's law proscribing circumcision and his order to rebuild Jerusalem as Aelia Capitolina and erect a temple to Jupiter Capitolinus (Zeus) on the site of the Jewish Temple. After three and a half years of guerilla warfare, Bar Kochba's last outpost fell. Jerusalem became the Roman colony Aelia Capitolina. The temple of Zeus was erected and Jews forbidden to enter it. The humiliation of the Jews was now complete. Almost two millenia would pass before they would return to their homeland. As important as the Temple was for their religious life, however, Judaism did not die. It did not die because its religious life revolved not only around the Temple but also around the Law.

Judaism's Institutions

Temple and Law figured prominently in the life of Jesus as in the life of every Jew. These were Judaism's two most important institutions, the focus not only of religious but also of political and social life. Indeed, no Jew would have thought to separate religion from all other aspects of life, here secular and there sacred. All of life was sacred. It involved a covenant with Yahweh.

So long as the Temple existed, it played an important part in the drama which portrayed and affirmed Israel's covenant relationship with their God. The first Temple was constructed by Solomon and lasted until the Exile. The Exile no doubt diminished the Jewish people's dependence upon the Temple as the central feature of worship and encouraged some reluctance to rebuild when the Exile ended officially. The prodding of Ezra and Nehemiah, however, resulted in a modest reconstruction. An even grander rebuilding took place under Herod the Great's sponsorship, beginning about 20/19 B. C. Despite these reconstructions, however, many surviving sources indicate that the Temple declined in importance between 200 B. C. and A. D. 70, so that the destruction of it in A. D. 70 caused less pain than one would expect.

Temple worship revolved around sacrifices. Sacrifices were offered to Yahweh publically both morning and evening. These were accompanied by lengthy and imposing ceremonies, followed by a detailed ritual and by many private sacrifices. Additional sacrifices were made on the Sabbath and feast days. These sacrifices, in theory, linked the celebrant to God. The act symbolized the covenant relationship between Yahweh and his people and the manifestation of Yahweh's actual presence in the midst of His people in the Temple.

Feast days marked off great "moments" in the history of salvation. Most festivals probably originated in agricultural observances, but they were historicized to coincide with great historical events. Three great festivals celebrated the divine mercy to Israel. *Passover* commemorated the deliverance of Israel from Egypt. It consisted not merely of public sacrifices but also of private home observances. Each family sought to enter into the event of the Exodus as if they had themselves gone through it. *Pentecost*, which in Greek means "fiftieth," came fifty days after Passover. More than any other festival, it retained its agricultural meaning wherein "first fruits" were offered in thanksgiving for the harvest. The *Feast of Tabernacles*, described as "the feast of ingathering, at the end of the year" (Exod. 23:16), was agricultural, but it also commemorated the wilderness wanderings of the Jewish people (Lev. 23:42-43). It was the last and greatest of the feasts, sometimes referred to as "the feast" *par excellence*. Besides these great festival days, the Jews had also a *Day of Atonement* in October (Lev. 16:23, 27-32; Num. 29:7-11). Its purpose was the cleansing of the sanctuary, priesthood, and people from sin and the re-establishment of the covenant between Yahweh and his people. In Maccabean days the Feast of Dedication was developed in order to set clear lines of commitment to the Law.

In Jesus' day the Temple service involved an immense number of persons. The Jewish historian Josephus estimated that the Temple staff consisted of 20,000. This staff was divided into twenty-four "courses," each responsible for service during one week. Each "course" included priests, Levites, and laymen. Officials included the high priest, the captain of the armed guard of the Temple, his inferior officers, heads of the twenty-four courses, priests and Levites, treasurers, porters, special functionaries charged with preparing the daily services, and musicians.

Control of the Temple lay in the hands of a hereditary priesthood, the descendents of the tribe of Levi. In the postexilic period this group assumed an ascendency which did not slacken until the reign of Herod the Great. Their place was elevated especially by the Hasmoneans.

The high priest, who maintained an exclusive control over the single altar in the Temple, was selected from a very small group of families. He had to be a descendent of Aaron. As the recognized mediator between Yahweh and the people, he was held in high esteem. Once nominated by the Sanhedrin, he underwent an elaborate seven day ritual of consecration. After consecration the Law hedged him about with special requirements concerning ritual purity.

As significant as the Temple was in Judaism, its destruction in A. D. 70 did not bring Israel's religious life to an end. The fact is, the Law had been waiting in the wings, as it were, so that it could move to the center of the stage. The shift began to crystallize about 400 B. C. as the scribal tradition grew at the expense of the sacerdotal.

The shift from Temple to Torah was momentous for the later history of Judaism. Torah stressed the personal element in religion and gave a· sense of cohesion, isolation from paganism, and power to withstand outside forces. It entailed a shift from ritual to observance and from sacrifices to good deeds.

Elevation of the significance of the Law in the religion of Israel necessitated the development of two ancillary institutions, the synagogue and the school. Little is known of their beginnings, but both of these were flourishing by 200 B. C. The aim of each was to educate the whole people in their religious traditions.

Synagogue worship focused upon reading and study of the scriptures, both the Law (the Pentateuch) and the prophets. Readings from the Pentateuch were prescribed according to the calendar. Selection of readings from the prophets was left to the reader, which explains why Jesus could choose the passage from Isaiah for his Nazareth synagogue sermon (Luke 4:17). Because Hebrew was no longer the language of the common person, these selections were translated or para-phrased — into Aramaic in Palestine and into Greek or other languages outside of Palestine. A homily on the passages read constituted the main portion of the service. But the latter also included recitation of the Shema (Deut. 6:4-5), prayers, benedictions, Psalm singing, and the use of certain liturgical formulas.

Synagogues came into existence wherever there were at

least ten Jewish men who could form an assembly. The general oversight of the synagogue rested with the elders, one of whose number was elected to be *Rosh ha-Keneset*, "head of the community." The latter presided, maintained order, and invited strangers to address the assembly. A salaried synagogue attendant, called a *Hazzan*, discharged a multitude of functions.

The *schools*, which were usually located next door to the synagogue, focused also on study of the scriptures. At age five the Jewish boy began by studying in a school which taught Hebrew. At age ten he advanced to a second school where he learned reading and writing. If he did well at these levels, he would study with a learned rabbi. At this level his study centered on tradition, called *Mishnah*.

One other institution also played a major part in the interpretation and application of the Law, that is, the *Sanhedrin*. The Sanhedrin probably originated in the days of Antiochus the Great (223-187 B. C.) when Jewish life suffered much from restrictions and probably needed some organization to regulate its internal affairs. Whom it consisted of originally is uncertain. However, there is evidence that it was first a *gerousia*, a body of elders, presided over by the high priest and consisting mainly of priests. It probably had some lay members as well, especially scribes or teachers of law, who gained considerable influence when Herod the Great became King. The Pharisees had little influence in it.

The Sanhedrin met in one of the chambers of the Temple. Composed of seventy or seventy-one members plus the high priest, it powers varied from time to time. The Romans restricted its functions in various ways. Politically it administered the criminal law, had independent police powers, including the right to make arrests, and judged non-capital offenses. In Jesus' day capital cases evidently required confirmation of the Roman Procurator. Religiously it supervised the Temple services and important ritualistic acts, such as the Day of Atonement, collected harvest tithes, judged cases of

adultery and passed sentence, arranged the calendar and provided correct copies of the Torah roll for King and Temple,
and decided doubtful questions of religious law, giving final
decisions in case of conflicting interpretations.

After the destruction of the Temple in A. D. 70 the Sanhedrin passed out of existence. Its functions then were
handed over to the Rabbinic school at Jamnia.

Parties and People

Although the Temple and the Law tended to create a sem-
blance of unity, especially from the Maccabean era on,
Judaism in the first century was by no means homogeneous.
There were numerous sects or parties which represented diverse political and religious perspectives and perceptions. Besides these, there were professional groups who seemed at
times to merge with one sect or another, for example, the
scribes with the Pharisees, and at times merely to represent
different specialties.

The two most influential parties, often described as opponents of one another, were the Sadducees and the Pharisees.
The Sadducees were concerned with the Temple, the Pharisees with the Law.

The name *Sadducees* probably came from "Zadokites,"
that is, descendents of Zadok, a priest of Solomon (1 Kings
2:35). Generally speaking, the Sadducees belonged to the
wealthy aristocracy. Accordingly, they were political conservatives. They may have accepted the concept of a Messiah,
but they did not favor the messianic expectations which excited the populace. Instead, they upheld the existing order,
whatever it was, so long as the religion of Israel was respected
and maintained.

The Sadducees were also religious conservatives and thus
clashed with the Pharisees on many views. In contrast to the
Pharisees, they acknowledged the Pentateuch alone as authoritative, interpreting it more literally and, in criminal
cases, less leniently than the Pharisees. Similarly they denied

the doctrines of resurrection, judgment, eternal life, and angels and demons, all of which the Pharisees accepted. They stressed free will and rejected the idea of Fate.

In the long run the entrenched conservatism of the Sadducees weakened their influence. Whereas the Pharisees claimed the authority of piety and learning, they claimed the authority of blood and position. Whereas the Pharisees strove to raise the standards of the masses, they lost themselves in Temple administration and ritual and ignored the masses. When the Temple was destroyed, they became a small sect without influence.

The *Pharisees* were evidently descendents of the *Hasidim*, the Jewish rebels who, when Antiochus Epiphanes proscribed Judaism in 168 B. C., preferred to die rather than violate the law and tradition of the elders by defending themselves on the sabbath (1 Macc. 2:29-38). Later they joined Judas Maccabeus in his fight against the Seleucids, but they withdrew in 164 B. C. when the war ended. Although the name "Pharisee," "separated," has been interpreted in several ways, it is clear that the chief characteristic of the party was zealous and scrupulous keeping of the Law.

Josephus first mentioned the Pharisees in connection with Jonathan, brother of Judas Maccabeus (161-143 B. C.). Their star rose and fell during the Hasmonean period, reaching a peak under Alexander Janneus (104-76 B. C.). During the reign of Herod the Great (37-4 B. C.), they lost much of their influence, but they regained it in the time of the Roman procurators. When the Jewish revolt failed in A. D. 70, they fled and, under leadership of Johanan ben Zakkai, established a school in Jamnia, in Palestine.

In this way they became leaders of the badly mauled Jewish people and helped Judaism to survive around study of the Law. Subsequently the school was moved to Usha, then Sepphoris, and then Tiberias. Later schools appeared in various places.

As indicated above, the Pharisees represented popular

opinion more than the Sadducees. Their basic contribution was the mediation of a knowledge of the Law to the people, their impressing of its authority upon them, and their setting an example of careful observance for them. Moreover, unlike the Sadducees, they advocated enlarging of the canon to include the prophets and the writings. They developed exegetical methods or rules in order to give a scriptural basis for any law or doctrine. And they counted both the written and the oral tradition authoritative. Doctrinally, in contrast to the Sadducees, they believed in the survival of the soul, the resurrection of the body, final judgment, and the life of the age-to-come. They emphasized divine forgiveness of sins on the basis of repentance. They also believed in angels and demons and looked for the imminent advent of the Kingdom of God. Regarding Jewish customs, they allowed new rites in the Temple and new festivals and favored the baptism of proselytes and a preparation of the Paschal meal.

Politically the Pharisees were progressive. Some of them at least shared the illusions of the Jewish nationalist movement, that is, concerning the survival of the Jewish state and its return to power. As a rule, they connected this hope more or less closely with the advent of a Messiah. Their chief concern, however, was to preserve the Jewish religion inviolable.

A third important party was the *Essenes*. Until recently, little precise information was available on them. In 1947, however, Judaean shepherds discovered a cave near the Dead Sea in which a hoard of manuscripts was found. Later exploration turned up several other manuscripts and manuscript fragments and the remains of a monastery thought to have been the home of the Essenes. These finds clarified immensely the fragmentary information supplied by Josephus, Philo, and some of the Church Fathers. Surprisingly, no New Testament writing alluded to the Dead Sea Covenanters, as they called themselves, possibly because many Essenes became members of the Church.

Like the Pharisees, according to this recent research, the

Essenes, if they were the same as the Dead Sea Covenanters, originated during the time of Antiochus Epiphanes' proscription of Judaism. Unlike the Pharisees, however, they were concerned less with the Law than with the Temple. They were protesting the profanation of the Temple by the official priesthood. They regarded themselves as the true priesthood, the "Sons of Aaron."

The Essenes imbibed strongly of Jewish apocalyptic expectations of the second century B. C. and after. They envisioned themselves as the Sons of Light preparing for the titanic battle with the Sons of Darkness. In accordance with this ideology, they arranged themselves in the fashion of a military hierarchy. They expected the victory to be achieved not so much by physical might as by the help of God's angels. They strove for complete separation from all evil ones, including the fallen in Israel, Temple priesthood and all. During the Jewish war, A. D. 66-70, they gradually decided that the battle of the last day was at hand. Armed with shovels and staves, they went out to meet the Romans, evidently the hated "Kittim" mentioned in their documents. Unfortunately for them the hosts of heaven did not show up. They were slaughtered mercilessly by the powerful Roman legions.

The Qumran Covenanters studied the Old Testament scriptures minutely, seeking clues to their own situation. According to some of their documents, members of the community studied in shifts around the clock. They evidently focused attention on prophetic elements in the scriptures and developed a method of interpretation by which ancient statements became types of their own history. They composed commentaries along such lines.

The Qumran Community was essentially monastic, with an inclination toward dualism. Although there may have been other communities with slightly differing characteristics, this community probably gives a fair picture of Essene beliefs and practices. The Essenes could have supplied early

Christianity with an important constituent core. They practiced community of goods. They fasted and observed a rigorous spiritual regimen. They had two sacramental rites — washing and observance of a sacred meal. These evidently symbolized their expectation of the coming of a Messiah. Candidates for admission went through a novitiate, or period of training in discipline. All members were subject to continuous scrutiny concerning their manner of life. Infractions evoked strong penalties. Organizationally, the community was hierarchically arranged. A council of twelve, including or plus three priests, made decisions which a Superintendent evidently executed. The whole community was organized in squads of ten with strict attention given to rank.

A striking number of points of agreement between these beliefs and customs and those of the early Christian Church has aroused speculation about the interrelationship between Qumran and the Church. The similarities are doubtless more than coincidental. They perhaps testify to a direct and significant impact effected by the conversion of many Essenes to Christianity. Moreover, it is quite possible that John the Baptist, Christianity's most important forerunner, was once a member of the Qumran sect. Certainly early Christians shared with John and the Essenes a powerful belief in messianic doctrines of Judaism.

Fascination with similarities, however, must not be allowed to obscure the differences between early Christianity and Qumran. While early Christianity shared in the excitement of Jewish messianic hopes, it did so from another angle; Christians believed that the long-awaited Messiah had come in Jesus of Nazareth. They were not merely looking forward to God's inbreak in history; they had seen it! Very quickly, moreover, they burst out of the grip of exclusivistic Judaism and incorporated Gentiles, so despised by the Essenes. Jesus taught not merely "Love your neighbor" but even "Love your enemy," something inconceivable for the Covenanters of Qumran.

Another important party was the *Zealots*. Although this sect may have been founded by Judas the Galilean mentioned in Acts 5:37, it had a prototype in the Maccabees with their zealous Jewish nationalism. Like the Maccabees, the Zealots were intense in their defense of Torah and Temple. Josephus seems to have been mistaken in identifying them with the Pharisees, for they probably drew members from several parties. They recognized God alone as Ruler and Lord and thus refused to recognize foreign rulers. They were concerned with the double scandal of godlessness among their compatriots and the subjugation of God's people to the yoke of foreigners.

Scholars are now debating the connection of Jesus with Zealots. The Twelve included at least one Zealot, an otherwise unknown disciple named Simon (Luke 6:15; Acts 1:13). Judas Iscariot may have had Zealot sympathies, a fact which would help to explain the betrayal. Judas may have betrayed Jesus out of disappointment that Jesus did not undertake to restore the nation. But what of Jesus himself? Was he put to death for Zealot activities, as a revolutionary? Did Christians then rewrite the story to make the Jews appear to be the culprits? Did they turn a revolutionary into a humble servant?

These questions have perhaps not been fully answered through a restudy of the early documents. It seems unlikely, however, that the first followers could have pulled off so grand a scheme of reinterpretation. Paul could call himself a Zealot (1 Cor. 14:12; Gal. 1:14), meaning a fighter to preserve his ancestral faith. As a Christian convert, however, he developed a completely new perspective, not to save Temple and Law but to bring a message of salvation to all people. It is too much to believe that Christianity underwent a complete metamorphosis between the death of Jesus and Paul's conversion, at most a space of five years.

A sect mentioned only twice in the Gospels (Mark 3:6; 12:13; Matt. 22:16) was the *Herodians*. They were hostile to Jesus. Presumably they were partisans of the family of

Herod, ruling at this time in Galilee and other areas but not in Judaea. The statement by later Christian writings that they regarded Herod as the Messiah is hardly more than speculation.

Sadducees, Pharisees, Essenes, Zealots, and Herodians represented the major sects or parties. In addition to these Judaism of Jesus' day depended upon several professional groups. From at least the time of the Chronicler (about 250 B. C.) there were guilds of priests, temple singers, and Levites. More important still were the scribes mentioned so often in the New Testament.

Although Ezra may have initiated the guild of scribes (Ezra 7:10f.), the profession came into its own between the acceptance of the Pentateuch (400 B. C.) as authoritative for Jewish faith and practice and the time of the Chronicler. Jesus ben Sirach, about 180 B. C., is the first known scribe. Scribes were often known by other names: *hakhamim* or wise men, rabbis, lawyers (Luke 2:46), and interpreters of the law.

Whereas priests saw that the Temple functioned properly, the scribes watched after the Law. At one time the priests may have handled interpretation, too, but as they yielded to political influence the scribes assumed a more important role. They were experts and specialists in interpretation. They instructed the young. They handed down decisions about the Law and about life in general.

At the time of Jesus the scribes were divided into two "schools" or traditions of interpretation — a strict and a liberal school. Followers of Rabbi Hillel emphasized neighborly love and a spirit of conciliation. Followers of Shammai stressed strict observance and the absolute authority of the Law and the jurisdiction of the scribes. The Shammaites, for example, forbade eating an egg laid by a hen on the Sabbath on the grounds that the hen worked. The Hillelites, per contra, allowed it on the grounds that the hen could not help laying the egg.

Scribes and Pharisees should not be confused with one

another. There were scribes who were not Pharisees and Pharisees who were not scribes. However, the Pharisees found support among the scribes for their concern about the Law.

Jewish Piety

A cursory reading of the New Testament may leave the false impression that Judaism possessed little genuine piety. At times Jesus seems virtually to have equated scribes and Pharisees as hypocrites (Matt. 23:13-15). He leveled serious charges of hypocrisy in the observance of prayers and fasts (Matt. 6:1ff.; Luke 12:56). He remonstrated the religious leaders for their casuistry and legalism by which they circumvented real obligations. Legalistic observance of tithes and the sabbath, for example, led to neglect of "weightier matters of the Law" (Matt. 23:23). The Corban rule allowed some to avoid paying due respect to parents (Matt. 7:11). Scribes and Pharisees traversed sea and land to make a proselyte to turn him into "twice as much a child of hell" as themselves (Matt. 23:15).

Whether such strong indictments accurately reflect Jesus' own sentiment is subject to question. Modern readers of the scriptures must remember certainly that the later strife between synagogue and church caused more critical statements to be preserved and often heightened. Jewish religion, therefore, often comes out looking worse than it was.

The fact is, in its best rather than in its worst light, Judaism of the New Testament era, especially the religion of the rabbis, merits much praise for its authentic desire to produce genuine piety. For persons who grew up within the Jewish matrix the many rules about fasting, tithing, sabbath observance, and all the rest were less irksome than they appear to moderns. Practiced from childhood, they became more or less habitual and automatic. The yoke of the Law did not have to be burdensome; rather, it could relieve the burden.

Those who probably chafed most under the regulations

were those called *Am Haarets*, "people of the land." The truly devout had to prod and cajole them. The *Am Haarets* operated at best in a minor key. It was the continuous concern of religious leaders to get such people keyed up about religious obligations, often to no avail.

The Sadducees may have taken religion casually, but the Pharisees and Essenes, as well as the scribes, took it seriously. They were zealous for faithfulness to the will of God. God's will, according to their understanding, had been revealed. It was embodied in the Law. Obedience to the Law meant obedience to God. By searching the scriptures, therefore, and applying them to everyday life, they were helping their fellows find God's will and live accordingly. The Apostle Paul's zeal for the Law and his claim of blamelessness as regards the righteousness which comes through it (Phil. 3:6) indicate the aim of Jewish piety.

Given such lofty aims, the Christian critique of Judaism may seem to stray completely from the target. What was wrong with it? Why did Christianity develop at all?

The weakness of Judaism, at least from the perspective of Paul as a convert to Christianity, lay in its strength. In zeal for righteousness the religion of the Pharisees had no peer. It was this zeal, however, which often encouraged neglect of divine grace. God, Paul discovered, is not a God of law but of grace. He extends his gracious love to all persons. All find justification before God not in their merit but in God's forgiveness and love. On that point, the scribes may have missed the central point of God's self-disclosure even in the Old Testament.

3

Jesus' World

Jesus spent his entire life in Palestine. Except for a brief excursion into Syria (Mark 7:24,31), which adjoined his native Galilee, he never left his homeland. With scanty exceptions he confined his ministry to the "house of Israel" (Matt. 15:24) and refused to allow his disciples to go beyond (Matt. 10:6).

Such facts as these might render the remarkable expansion of early Christianity all but incomprehensible if one did not remember that Rome and Hellenism cast their spell over most of the ancient Mediterranean world. Jesus did not go to Rome, it is true, but Rome came to his homeland, and with it came Hellenism with its penchant for absorbing and assimilating elements of culture. Rome and Hellenism were a providential preparation for the spread of Christianity from Jerusalem through Judaea and Samaria to the "uttermost parts of the earth." Rome and Romans figured prominently in Jesus' mission and message. They figured even more prominently in the spread of the movement he founded.

Rome and Romanitas

When Jesus was born, the Roman Empire was still growing. It did not reach its maximum extent until the reign of the Emperor Hadrian, about 115 A. D.

Continuous expansion brought with it massive administrative problems within as well as military problems without. The long range solution to both sets of problems was centralization. In the time of Octavian (31 B. C. - A. D. 14) Rome was in transition from a republic to an empire. The transition took place gradually, not being consummated until Diocletian assumed the title of *Dominus* in 285. Octavian himself accepted the title of *princeps* and additional grants of power from the Roman Senate with some reluctance. He refused divine honors in Rome, though he evidently conceded to popular ascriptions in the provinces. At the same time Julius Caesar was posthumously deified. Emperor worship reinforced the trend toward centralization. Subsequent emperors made increasing claims of divine honors, thus setting up the inevitable conflict with Christian claims.

The age of Augustus was looked upon by Roman literati like Vergil as a golden age. In some respects that may have been true; in others it was not. The Empire was characterized by vast economic and social contrasts, similar in many ways to those one finds in the United States today.

Rome's conquests created a cosmopolitan character. Yet at the same time there was much provincialism even in the city of Rome. The bounties of the Empire flowed toward the eternal city more than they flowed outward toward the provinces.

The population centered in great cities — Antioch, Alexandria, Ephesus, Carthage, Rome. Rome itself had nearly a million inhabitants. Such cities brought cultural and social advantages — art, music, games, baths, and many others. Already in the first century, however, the metropolises were developing the same problems modern cities face — water supply, food supply, sanitation, housing, overcrowding, unemployment, security, etc. It is highly likely that the half-mad Emperor Nero had urban renewal in mind when, in A. D. 64, he set fire to the city of Rome and then used Christians as scapegoats for his ill-devised scheme.

The Empire was noted for vast wealth of individuals and

the poverty of masses. The wealthy lived in grand villas and fled the noise, filth and clutter of the cities. They enjoyed all the necessities and many of the luxuries of life. They lived in opulently furnished and decorated homes. They had elegant private baths with water ranging from steaming hot to icy cold. They were waited on hand and foot by slaves. Some of them were the old aristocracy, but many represented a new breed who had arisen through the ranks of the army or by other means to positions of power and influence.

The masses, among whom early Christianity reaped its early harvest, enjoyed few of these benefits. For them there was a daily struggle for existence. They lived in dread of conscription for the army. They feared loss of property and belongings. They groaned under heavy taxation. They agonized over problems of family and child rearing very much as moderns do. Literacy varied, but only a limited number could read and write well. Some signed legal papers with an "X". There was despair in the face of sickness and death.

During the first century, too, people grew more and more dependent on state maintenance. Rome and Romans exhibited a remarkable largesse. Wealthy persons sought to outdo one another in lavishing favors upon both equals and the less fortunate. They erected public buildings, constructed aqueducts and sanitary systems, built baths and gymnasia, paved streets and roads, sponsored religious and public festivals, paid for and distributed grain, oil and other commodities, gave handouts of cash and clothing, purchased freedom for slaves, adopted orphans, supplied scholarly stipends for needy students, and rendered a multitude of other services to their fellow men. Emperors footed immense bills for "bread and circuses." In Rome especially they let the public stores overflow with virtual abandon. So costly did the monthly grain allotment become that the Emperor Octavian restricted it to 200,000 and later 150,000 citizens. The emperors conciliated and curried the favor of a sometimes unruly populace with public fetes and games, which became an absolute necessity as time passed. They set an example for their provincial governors, public administrators, and other wealthy citizens in erecting fine new public buildings, in rebuilding cities leveled by fires and earthquakes, or other natural disasters, in constructing magnificent harbors, public baths, sanitary systems, and in otherwise adding to the amenities of life. The fabulous range of public construction by Herod the Great offers but one instance of the spirit which imperial benefactions infused into others.

In all, however, Rome's achievements in the early Christian era were grandiose rather than great. Nothwithstanding its vast power, Rome did little to embue its citizens with a feeling of security. There was a growing pessimism, a developing sense of sin, a loss of self-confidence and hope, a despair of patient inquiry, an indifference to the welfare of the state coupled with expanding individualism, and loneliness. All of these developments encouraged asceticism, mysticism, a cry for infallible revelation, and longing for conversion. All kinds of religious interests thrived. So did superstitions — consulting augurers and soothsayers, carrying magical papyri, wearing charms and amulets, and worshipping the dead.

Moral and ethical standards varied. Stoic philosophers set a fine example with their ethics of enlightened self-interest. Numerous people, especially at the upper cultural levels, displayed admirable social perceptions and patterns of personal morality. The common people, however, struggling to survive, did not act so commendably. The sources tell the usual tales of sexual profligacy, theft, rape, murder, and the like. Infanticide was common where unwanted children, especially girls, came along. Women, children, and slaves were not accorded equal status.

Alongside increasing brutality grew a humanitarian sensitivity. Many tired of the butchery which transpired in the arenas in the form of gladiatorial combats, animal fights, and chariot races. They were wearied by constant warfare. Nevertheless, such things continued, and the appetite of the masses for them grew rather than diminished.

Hellenism

The fact that Rome held this vast, disparate Empire together for several centuries is little short of miraculous. This was a consequence of several things: First, it was due in part to the Roman military prowess. To that time the Roman army was one of the best equipped, trained, disciplined, and commanded ever put on the field. Second, it was due to the strength of Roman organization and administration. The Empire was divided into numerous provinces, structured on military lines, and put in the hands of capable Roman or native governors and kings. So long as these appointees ruled wisely and effectively, the emperors interfered little. If a subordinate failed, he bore full responsibility and suffered accordingly. The powerful Roman army, stationed in each province, could move quickly and decisively to quell riots and to restore the civil peace. Third, it was due to Roman technology, aided by an unlimited supply of slave labor. A network of excellent highways connected all parts of the Empire. A postal system maintained relatively rapid lines of communication between Rome and the far flung military outposts and provincial capitals. A strong supply fleet kept grain and other supplies flowing from Egypt and agricultural areas to Rome.

Beyond these factors, however, the most powerful cement of all was the pervasive spirit of Hellenism. Rome, after all, was not a disseminator of the spirit of Rome so much as of the spirit of Greece. Greek culture enthralled the Romans as much as it had other ancient peoples. As Rome conquered the remains of the empire of Alexander of Macedon, Hellenism conquered Rome. In the final analysis, Hellenism contributed more than any of the other complex factors to the unity of the Empire and to the Empire's part in the spread of early Christianity. It did so in several ways:

One was linguistic. Greek, in the popular version known as *Koine*, was the universal language of the Empire. To be sure, native tongues and dialects, for example, Aramaic in Palestine, still remained the first language of captured peoples. Moreover, Greek did not penetrate to remote rural areas. It did become, however, the means by which persons from as far east as Babylon and as far west as the British Isles would carry on conversation and commerce. Language posed no insuperable barrier to human intercourse.

Another was a common world view, one handed down from Plato and emphasizing the unity of all things. This world view was incorporated into various philosophies and philosophical systems — Stoicism, Pythagoreanism, Platonism — and it had a unitive effect even on them. According to this world view, all things emerged out of one, a world soul or mind. Thus all strive toward unification with the one. Ultimately all will be reunited.

Another was a love of Greek customs and ideas. The peoples who came under the Roman banner were united not merely by language and world view but by sharing customs in dress, physical exercise, education, architecture, and many other things. The Jews in Palestine remained almost alone in their antipathy to Hellenistic culture. Outside Palestine, as indicated earlier, even Jews became thoroughly Graecized. Jesus' contemporary Philo of Alexandria read Plato's philosophy into the Pentateuch, thus preparing the way for Christian apologists. He contended that the best of Hellenism was borrowed from Moses and could be seen in Moses' writings if the latter were carefully studied. Other Jews imitated Greek art and architecture. They adopted Greek dress. They aped Greek ways. The spirit of Hellenism prevailed.

The Religions of Rome

When the Apostle Paul characterized his hearers in Athens as in every way "very religious" (Acts 17:22), he fittingly depicted citizens of the Roman Empire. The Romans *were* "very religious." They were convinced that Rome had become great not merely because of the gods but because of their devotion to the gods. This devotion took several forms.

Officially it took the form of the carefully prescribed rites and rituals of the state cultus. The state cultus was a hodge podge of elements drawn from various sources. It went back to the religion of early tribes which originally inhabited the Italian peninsula and which emphasized war. At an early date it came under the influence of the Greek religions, the Roman deities being little more than Olympian gods with Roman names. The three chief deities were Juppiter (Greek Zeus), Mars (god of war), and Minerva. Besides them, there were the goddesses of fertility, goddesses of the flocks and herds, and twelve special gods who discharged various functions. Later on, Roman religion underwent open Hellenization.

The formalized and stereotyped character of the state cultus made it unattractive to the masses. An attempted reform under Augustus did little to revive it, although the development of emperor worship introduced an important new twist. Emperor worship, like so many other features of Roman religion, also was an inheritance from Greece. Greek heroes were viewed as divinities. Alexander the Great was hailed as "a god" upon his entry into Egypt in 332 B. C. by a priest of Isis. Alexander's successors, both Ptolemies and Seleucids, claimed divine honors. Then, more than a century before the Empire began, the Roman state was deified. It was natural, therefore, to expect the emperor to receive the same ascription as a personification of the state.

Julius Caesar claimed divine honors, but the Senate did not declare this until after his death. In Ephesus a temple was erected "to the goddess *Roma* and the divine Julius." Octavian forbade the proclamation of divine honors in Rome, but in 29 B. C. sanctioned it in the erection of a temple in Ephesus and in accepting the title Augustus. The totally mad Caligula (37-41) was the first, however, to demand universal homage to his statue. Domitian (81-96) was the first to use real force to sustain the emperor cult. To subordinates he was *deus et dominus* (God and Lord).

To the average Roman citizen the rites of the state cultus were purely perfunctory, a pledge of allegiance. He felt attracted much more strongly to the oriental cults which were moving westward and becoming intermixed with the spirit of Hellenism. One of these was *Judaism*, which, despite its exclusivism, attracted many Romans who had a serious interest in its monotheism, high moral standards, and historical promises. Adolf Harnack, 19th Century German historian of Dogma, once estimated that in the first century Jews and Jewish converts composed as much as seven percent of the Roman populace.

A second was *Cybele*, the first cult installed in Rome from east of the Hellespont. Although admitted only as a foreign cult in 205 B. C., by the time of Augustus' reform it had become firmly entrenched. Originally a wild, enthusiastic religion characteristic of Phrygia, it was modified by merger with Greek and Roman cults, especially the cult of Attis. In place of earlier orgiastic rites appeared the mythology of a self-mutilated and restored god which promised the worshipper rebirth and immortality. Much of its attractiveness doubtless lay in its priesthood and colorful pageantry. Even women were allowed to hold the priestly office. The rank and file formed corporations through which they could enjoy social fellowship without regard to status and rank.

The purified worship of later times consisted of dramatic portrayals of the legends of Cybele and Attis. A week long spring festival, obviously capitalizing on nature symbolism, depicted over several days the multilation-restoration myth. The gradual transformation of the cult of Cybele led to the adoption of the rite of *taurobolium*, a bath in bull's blood, during the second century. By this bloody baptism, it was believed, "buried" in the pit with accompanying rites, the devotee was purified of his sins and raised to a new life.

A third was *Isis and Osiris*, an Egyptian cult which was

propagated with considerable modification in the Greek world by the Ptolemies. By the agency of travelers, sailors, slaves, artisans, popular writings, and even soldiers it spread all over the Roman Empire. About A. D. 215 Caracalla submitted to its inevitable public recognition by building an Iseon on the Quirinal hill in the heart of Rome.

The genius of the Isis-Osiris cult lay in its ability to adapt easily to the different milieux where it was transported and to become "all things to all men." At the popular level it possessed two powerfully attractive features: a myth that assured devotees of immortality and an appealing liturgy. The myth concerned the death and resuscitation of the young god Osiris, who reputedly civilized Egypt. Osiris was hacked to pieces by the jealous Typhon, and the pieces were scattered. But Osiris' wife, Isis, searched until she found each part, excepting the male member, and held a funeral for the body. Subsequently Osiris returned to life and came back periodically to be with his wife and son.

This romantic myth came to life in the dramatic worship of the cult. The worship consisted both of daily rites and significant annual festivals, plus the private devotions of the faithful. According to Egyptian belief the gods needed to be fed, dressed, and refreshed every day. For this purpose the Isis cult developed a fixed ritual entailing much pomp. Besides these impressive daily rituals, there were two major festivals. The first, observed on March 5 to celebrate the reopening of the seas at the end of the winter months, involved a magnificent processional to the river, where the goddess Isis, protector of sailors, could bless the water. The other, celebrated from October 26 to November 3, portrayed the "Finding of Osiris." In this most moving of all ceremonies, the cult portrayed the god falling under the blows of Set (Typhon?) as he left the temple. The worshippers simulated funeral lamentations around the body. Then Horus, Osiris' son, overcame Set, and Osiris, who had returned to life, entered his temple after his victory over death.

The Isis-Osiris cult also had an impressive initiation ceremony. The central part of the rite is not known, but, thanks to Apuleius, the preparatory rites for it are. Paralleling the pre-baptismal rites of Christianity, the latter included instruction in certain esoteric writings, bodily ablutions, and fasting for ten days. Whatever the initiation rite consisted of, it made a profound impression upon those initiated. According to Lucius in Apuleius' *Metamorphoses,* "about midnight I saw the sun brightly shine, I saw likewise the gods celestial and the gods infernal, before whom I presented myself and worshipped them." In the morning the newly initiated emerged to stand before the goddess, lighted torch in hand and garland of flowers with white palm leaves sticking out like rays of the sun on his head. After the public revelation the whole congregation celebrated his "birth of sacred things" with two days of ceremonies and banquets.

A fourth was *Mithra,* fundamentally a Persian dualistic sect. It struck root in the West during the Flavian era and by the mid-third century, particularly through its attractiveness to soldiers on the frontier, appeared on its way to nearly universal acceptance. In its westward trek it experienced considerable modification both by semitic and hellenistic contacts, but much less than the Isis-Osiris cult. It exhibited remarkable likenesses to Christianity both in theology and practice and its appeal to both the intellect and the conscience, which many other cults lacked, made it a serious rival of Christianity. The initiation of Commodus had immense influence subsequently, so that Mithra virtually eclipsed its rivals. In the year 307 Diocletian, Galerius, and Licinius consecrated a sanctuary at Carnuntum on the Danube to Mithra, "protector of the Empire," and the Emperor Julian made Mithra the center of his pagan revival. Such evidences led Ernest Renan to the conclusion that "Had Christianity not triumphed, Mithra would have." Such a conclusion is debatable, however, for Mithraism excluded women, thus eliminating a sizeable portion of its potential constituency.

Mithra had a powerful moral emphasis, which, like that of

Judaism and early Christianity, harked back to the ancient Irano-Persian idea of a perpetual struggle between the god of light, Ormuzd, and the god of darkness, Ahriman. Life was viewed in this theology as a continuous battle between good and evil, the gods (angels) and demons. Mithra, one of the lesser deities in Zoroastrian thought, but identified with the *Sol Invictus* in Roman, exemplified the true soldier of light and allied himself with man.

The Mithraic system fostered individual effort to resist evil and to do good. The faithful, soldiers of Mithra, must constantly oppose the demonic powers by self-discipline. At death, it was believed, souls stained by evil would be seized by the emissaries of Ahriman and dragged down to the depths of hell to suffer indescribable tortures. On the other hand, the pure would be borne aloft to the celestial realm where the supreme god, Kronos (Ormuzd), reigned, passing through the seven planetary spheres guarded over by angels of Ormuzd. The initiate of Mithra alone would know how to satisfy these guardians and thereby penetrate to the eighth heaven. Mithra himself would serve as their guide. At the end, after a general resurrection, he would judge all humanity separating good from bad once-for-all. Then the great god would cause fire to fall from heaven and consume the wicked spirits, including Ahriman, and an age of eternal blessedness would dawn.

Mithraism possessed an organization and rites quite similar to Christianity's. The adherents formed associations or brotherhoods. According to Jerome, famous Palestinian monk and biblical scholar of the late fourth and early fifth centuries, there were seven grades of initiation. Besides or above these there were apparently priests, ranked in a kind of hierarchy with a chief priest, called "father of the fathers," at the top, and ascetics and virgins. Among Mithraic rites the most important were the *taurobolium*, repeated ablutions to wash away guilty stains, branding or sealing (apparently behind the right ear), pouring of honey on hands and tongue in initiation to the lion class after a long novitiate, and a meal consisting of bread and water mixed with wine, symbolizing the gift of power to combat evil spirits and of immortality. In addition to these significant rites the Mithra cult maintained a regular schedule of worship, but information about this is quite fragmentary. Each day of the week was devoted to a planet, but Sunday had particular significance. Certain calendrical observances were held, too, the most notable being the festival in honor of the Unconquered Sun on December 25, which about 335 became the date on which Christians observed Jesus' birth.

In what has been said about Mithraism, one cannot fail to notice the closeness of the similarities to Christianity. This was doubtless due to some interchange of ideas and observances between these competing religions, but it was due also to their common heritage from both East and West. Both religions were affected markedly by Irano-Persian views. However, one may see also in the dominant Jewish inheritance of Christianity where the rivals began to part the ways. In respect of monotheism Christianity stood firm with Judaism; it tolerated no compromise with idolatry. But, somewhat surprisingly in view of the firm position adopted here, it also proved better suited to respond to the demands imposed upon it by pagan culture than Mithraism. Where the latter superficially loaded itself with an abundance of gross superstitions in adapting to western culture without really assimilating them into its total structure, Christianity refined and remolded what it could approve to bring it in line with its monotheistic covenant faith.

Philosophies

Neither the state cultus nor the religions of the orient satisfied all persons. The privileged and well educated turned instead to the philosophies. They could do so comfortably even when exploring religious issues because the philosophies devoted much of their attention to religion; they were, in fact, religions as much as philosophies. Philosophers became preachers of faith and morality. In the first century or so of the Christian era Stoicism excited the interest and captured the allegiance of most philosophically oriented persons; from the mid-second century on Platonism of one type or another prevailed.

The principal concern of philosophical religion was morality. In consequence, the Stoics fashioned a system with a highly ethical concern; in fact, it contributed rather significantly to the structuring of early Christian ethical theory. The two Stoic giants of the first and second centuries, the Roman jurist Seneca and Epictetus, a one time slave turned philosopher, made conduct, as T. R. Glover observed, "nine-tenths of life." Before all other things they challenged men to live in accord with Nature, thereby experiencing emancipation from the world and harmony with the divine. "Not to stray from Nature and to mold ourselves to her law and example," Seneca said in his treatise *On the Blessed Life*, "is genuine wisdom." The divine is within us and happiness depends upon *apatheia*, inner self-detachment. The happy man will care neither for pleasure nor pain. Virtue will be his sole pursuit. "Would you propitiate the gods?" asked Seneca. "Be good! Whoever has imitated them has worshipped them enough."

This type of philosophy obviously supplied a deficiency of traditional Roman religion in its concern for the individual. Its decline after the time of Epictetus (ca. A. D. 50-130), however, demonstrates that Stoicism too was found wanting. In its individualism lay an unrealistic conception of human nature, which, like Pelagianism, a fifth century Christian heresy which emphasized man's free will, did not take seriously enough the connection of man with humanity. The Stoic sage was himself isolated from the common man. Lifted up to the level of an intellectual and spiritual elite who stood aloof from the vulgar crowd, he had only a vague grasp of the situation of those teeming masses who must live by grace, knowing full well they can never measure up to their own expectations, much less those of God. The doctrine of *apatheia* especially reveals a gross underestimation of the power of human passions. In the end the happiness promised by Seneca and Epictetus could have been the possession of a very few. As Stoicism bared its deficiencies, increasingly syncretistic systems appeared, suiting well a tendency of the age. A kind of religious revival sprang up around the teachings of Plutarch of Chaeronea (ca. A. D. 46-after 120), who amalgamated philosophy, tradition, and law or custom in one grand religious and moral system. Making Platonism his foundation he constructed his edifice with tidbits borrowed from philosophers, poets, legislators, hellenic and barbarian religions, mysteries, oracles, private utterances — the whole complex Graeco-Roman civilization. In conscious opposition to the Epicureans and Stoics, who sounded a skeptical note regarding religion, Plutarch believed that the latter was the underpining of all law and the cohesive for all society. Thence he condemned the Stoics for turning the gods into natural forces. Tradition, oracles, and mysteries, he insisted, all verify the gods' existence.

Plutarch, following Hesiod, a Greek poet of the eighth century B. C. known as the father of didactic poetry, worked out a complete hierarchy of rational creatures not unlike the early Christian: the Ultimate God — deputy gods — demons — men. The deputy gods and demons formed the center of his theological system, for, like the Neoplatonists later, he struggled with the problem of bridging the gap between the One and the many, good and evil. Demons, who have a mixed nature, solved the problem of mediation between God and the (deputy) gods, who are pure, on the one hand, and men, who also have a mixed nature, on the other. These demons fulfill a dual role, actually, some bearing responsibility for evil and some supplying man's higher needs. As regards the latter purpose, which Plutarch dwelled on most of the time, they aid souls to gain freedom from the body, not just any soul, of course, but those which strive to detach themselves from the welter of worldly affairs. Corrupt souls may perish, Plutarch has a companion say in one treatise, but God sends a demon to lend aid to those who strive to reach the upper world.

With this system of demons who communicate freely with men Plutarch ameliorated the less pleasing aspects both of pagan philosophy and religion while retaining some of their better features. He criticized severely popular superstition, which in his judgment sowed the seeds for atheism. He demythologized the legends of the mystery cults in order to bring their theistic views into line with philosophy. He created a doctrine of Providence which took into account both the universal power of the divine and the free will of man. Although his polytheism left ample room for criticism, his synthesis of so many diverse elements in the Hellenistic milieu proved sufficiently appealing to give the experiment a considerable period of success.

Demonolatry and Gnosis

Whatever significant elements in Roman religion and philosophy have escaped notice in the preceding, they can best be captured in a study of demonolatry. Belief in and dread of demons stood at the center of religious observance from the first century of the Christian era on. "It is probably not too hard a thing to say," Charles Bigg observed in *The Church's Task Under the Roman Empire*, "that demon worship was the really operative religion of the vast mass of the population of the Empire."

The cult of demons received support from Neoplatonic philosophy, which, in its popular form, was strongly inclined toward the religio-philosophical tendency or movement now known as *Gnosis* or Gnosticism. The well known classical Neoplatonism of Plotinus (ca. 205-270) by no means represented the mainstream. Most Neoplatonists, on the contrary, followed in the steps of Plutarch in developing an elaborate theory of intermediate spiritual beings by which popular piety could be defended and the problem of one and many, good and evil, solved in the process. Celsus, Maximus of Tyre, Porphyry, and Iamblichus, among others, developed a kind of "spiritualism," in which the demons represented spiritual forces at work in the operation of the universe but were at the same time personal.

The syncretistic process witnessed in Plutarch, Celsus, and Maximus reached a peak during the third century in a popular amalgamation of solar monotheism, polytheism, and various superstitions. Although both Porphyry (232/3-ca. 305) and Iamblichus (ca. 250-ca. 325) could be adduced in evidence of this, the same phenomenon is equally well attested in the diverse writings assembled in the *Corpus Hermeticum*. Composed and edited at various times between the second and fourth centuries, the latter provide an illuminating, even if confused picture of a popular Neoplatonic-Gnostic combination of philosophy and religion. One sees in these compositions the basic Platonic world view modified by Stoicism, Neopythagoreanism, (itself an amalgam of various earlier philosophies), astrology, the mystery cults, Christianity, popular superstition, and a mass of other elements.

A consistent theme of these preacher-philosophers was salvation through *gnosis*, i.e. "knowledge." As in Christian Gnosticism, a combined Greek and oriental dualism formed the foundation of their redemptive schemata. God, the One, alone is good. The world is "one mass of evil." Man's body, therefore, is also evil, being material. Only by apprehending God can the soul apprehend the Good; therefore, it must seek *gnosis* of God. *Gnosis*, spiritual and not intellectual knowledge, leads to rebirth, a new manner of life. To know God one must strip off his "cloak of evil," i.e. the body, and in this way see God. The main vice of any man is lack of *gnosis*, the main virtue *gnosis*.

Ultimately redemption involves a return of the soul to God. At death the material body dissolves. The vital principle (soul) ascends through the seven planetary spheres above the earth, stripping off as it does the vices which those spheres imposed in the descent of the first Man. Having thus purged itself, the soul enters the eighth sphere and joins the "Powers" who continually sing God's praises. Thus each soul which has obtained *gnosis*, the true virtue, mounts up to God and itself becomes one of the "Powers."

Demons play a significant role in man's life and salvation throughout the *Corpus Hermeticum*. An "avenging demon" is given charge of evil, ignorant souls who do not know God, and he punishes and casts them down further in their self indulgence. Evil demons inhibit the performance of good. Human souls, if good, "change into (good) demons, and thereafter pass on into the choral dance of the gods." Book XVI, dated in the third century, outlines a complete heavenly hierarchy similar to Plutarch's, and offers a lucid testimony of the advanced demonology of the day.

An idea of an omnipresent troop of intermediate divine beings opened a way for sustaining the continuance of many essentially primitive religious practices. On this basis, as one example, Celsus, Maximus, and Iamblichus all defended the offering of *sacrifices*. Even greater interest lay, as a second example, in the defense of *divination* in its many aspects. The widespread belief in the doctrine of fate (*heimarmene*) elevated greatly the significance of various media of divination, which many Neoplatonists proceeded to defend. The latter undergirded their thinking by citing the "demon" of Socrates. Iamblichus drew the logical conclusion from his predecessors and sustained every imaginable form of divination — dreams, ecstatic trances, enthusiasm, oracles, prophetic illumination, private inspirations, examination of viscera, watching birds, star-gazing, and even examination of the inanimate — pebbles, rods, pieces of wood, stones, corn, wheat. Though he conceded the evils in divination, he insisted that the erroneous could be distinguished from the true by checking its correspondence with the nature of the gods.

If such thinking as this characterized the chief representatives of Neoplatonism, one can readily guess how the average man viewed life. He resided in a world alive with both beneficent and maleficent beings. Every bush and tree, every rock and pebble, every grove and forest was the probable lurking place of demons. With limited powers of discrimination the common person could easily identify these with the ancient gods, with nymphs and satyrs, with ancestral shades, or with any number of mythological heroes and villains. The demons, he believed, controlled his behavior and determined his destiny. What mattered to him was whether he could propitiate the bad and enlist the good on his side.

In light of this conception of their existence one is not surprised to learn that the masses did obeisance to the appropriate powers in strange ways. They carried texts, offered sacrifices, made secret signs, consulted soothsayers and augurers, searched horoscopes, composed poems and songs, prayed, fasted, gave votive offerings, probed the entrails of birds and animals, went on pilgrimages to holy shrines, undertook arduous tasks, erected monuments to the gods with appropriate inscriptions — all in the name of fearful unknown. Multitudes went off after miracle workers, like Apollonius of Tyana, a first century Pythagorean philosopher and world traveler. They became the prey of magicians, miracle-mongers, pseudo-prophets, and religious quacks like Alexander of Abonoteichus, a devotee of Aesculapius, god of healing. By various devices, according to Lucian of Antioch, Alexander stirred up great fervor for his deity and attracted people from far and wide with predictions of the future, oracles, and claims to discover runaway slaves, detect thieves, find treasures, heal the sick, and even raise the dead. Thousands expended fortunes on magic. A lengthy magical papyrus in the British Museum describes a plethora of magical formulas and spells: for curing coughs and headaches, for protection against danger, for summoning another person to come immediately, for procuring a personal appearance of the deity, for obtaining information about the present and the future, for inciting visions and dreams, for making someone reveal secrets in his sleep, for attracting the love of another, for divine protection and aid against other persons or against demons and apparitions or against illness, for producing sleeplessness, for causing a shadow in the sun by which information could be secured, and so on *ad nauseam.*

Christianity's Task

Christianity, therefore, began with a formidable challenge. Along with the other religions and philosophies, it had the imposing task of humanizing the occult and of eliminating the dread of the divine so that a genuine encounter between God and man could take place. In many respects, it had to discharge the tasks of both science and religion. The pretended popular science of the day, astrology and magic and divination, did exactly the reverse: they capitalized upon man's ignorance and fears in order to enhance their own reputations and, quite often, for the sake of personal gain. Many religious cults perhaps did the same.

Little in Christianity's beginnings looked promising. Its founder was crucified as a common criminal in an obscure corner of the Empire. For a century and a half Christianity barely survived and scarcely received notice among the cultured, consequential people of the Empire. When it did, it had a bad press. Its competitors, especially the other oriental cults, appeared to have the upper hand, for they obtained at least a little legal sanction. Still Christianity did survive. It survived and it grew. By the time Constantine adopted it as his own faith it claimed ten to fifteen percent of the Roman populace. By the time of the Roman Emperor Theodosius (379-395) it was illegal not to be Christian. Soon after, imperial suppression eliminated all competitors. None of the competitors could withstand opposition as Christianity had.

There may be no answer to the intriguing question: Why did Christianity and not one of its competitors, philosophy or religion, triumph? Any attempted answer surely is complex. Part of it, at least, lies with the founder of Christianity — his life and ministry, his teaching, his death, and, above all, the conviction of his first followers that he had been raised from the dead.

PART TWO

"The Fullness of Time"

4

The Life and Ministry
of Jesus

Some scholars would dispute the implication of the title of this chapter. It is their contention that the sources, being mostly Christian and of such nature as to evoke faith, will not allow one to reconstruct Jesus' life in any manner. Jesus thus should be viewed as a presupposition for Christian theology and history, not as the historical founder of Christianity.

Behind this view lies a considerable history of New Testament studies, especially in Germany. In the early nineteenth century German liberal scholarship turned Jesus into a German rationalist. Rationalistic interpretations were followed by mythological ones, in which, beginning with David Friedrich Strauss, doubt was cast on Jesus' actual existence. Next appeared liberal lives which substantiated Jesus' historicity but reduced his teaching to the fatherhood of God and brotherhood of man and his mission to the establishment of an earthly kingdom. This view was severely challenged by a series of studies which demonstrated Jesus' essentially eschatological orientation, that is, his expectation of the inbreak of God's kingdom and with it the consummation of his purposes for mankind. The eschatological lives, particularly Albert Schweitzer's *Quest of the Historical Jesus*, posed anew the question: How much can be known about Jesus? The development of form criticism as a method of New Testament study demonstrated more fully the difficulty of constructing a biography. Form criticism revealed a process of oral transmission before the composition of the canonical Gospels in which most data about Jesus are found. Form critics viewed the Gospels, previously thought chronologically arranged, as collections of sayings, miracle stories, parables, etc. arranged according to particular concerns of their authors. Even Mark, which provided the framework for Matthew and Luke, was adjudged to be more or less useless for chronology. Like the others, Mark too wrote the story with his own slant and with little chronological interest.

Despite these developments, New Testament scholars did not abandon altogether the search for a historical framework for the life and ministry of Jesus. English scholars such as T. W. Manson and C. H. Dodd remained convinced that Mark contained a more or less reliable framework. Dodd went further to argue that this framework was conserved in the earliest preaching of the Christian missionaries and that Mark incorporated that into his Gospel. After thorough critical study Vincent Taylor concluded that Jesus' ministry could be outlined in four or five stages: (1) a pre-Galilean ministry, (2) a Galilean ministry, (3) a withdrawal from Galilee, (4) a Jerusalem ministry, and (5) the passion and resurrection. This would not qualify as a biography, but it does give credence to Jesus as a historical personage.

In recent years German scholars have shown signs of interest in what is called "a new quest of the historical Jesus." Although the distinguished Marburg professor Rudolf Bultmann remained skeptical, several of his students have opened the possibility of writing a "life" which would be consistent with the radically changed modern understanding of history and human existence. Such a "life" would not attempt a chronicle or *curriculum vitae* but an interpretation of Jesus. It would focus on his self-understanding.

Many contemporary studies have encouraged this kind of reassessment. During the twentieth century advances have taken place in areas which aid the quest for a new "life." One is background studies in the history of New Testament times, other religions, the geography of Palestine, archeology, the Aramaic language, rabbinic literature and thought, and apocalyptic literature and thought. Another is studies of the sources, especially John and the Synoptists (Matthew, Mark, and Luke). Another is development of different social perceptions, for example, in the social gospel movement.

The Sources

The fervor of this debate, past and present, makes it wise to say more about the sources for discussing Jesus' life and ministry. From what has been said thus far it will be evident that the four Gospels contained in the New Testament supply most of the material. All four of these have to be seen not as biographies but as theological writings which bear witness first of all to the faith of the early Church.

The theological tendency of the Gospel according to John has long been recognized. John's prologue makes clear that he was not giving a day by day, week by week resume of Jesus' life but was interpreting theologically. Since the beginning of the modern critical era, scholars have used John cautiously and sparingly to reconstruct Jesus' ministry. Some have given little credence to information contained only in John. More recently, however, others have reassessed some data in John's favor, for instance, concerning Jesus' visit to Judaea before the Galilean ministry began.

The theological tendencies of the other three Gospels were recognized more slowly. In some ways this is surprising, for the content of each of them readily betrays some theological slant. Mark, for example, regarded by many as the earliest Gospel, omitted any mention of Jesus' birth and early years. In addition, he opened with a revealing title, "The beginning of the gospel of Jesus Christ, the Son of God." Then he proceeded to tell the story in terms of a gradual self-disclosure by Jesus of his messianic role.

Matthew and Luke both contain genealogies designed to trace Jesus' descent from David and both include virgin birth narratives. Each, however, has a different theological slant. Matthew, evidently addressing a Jewish audience, continually pointed out how Jesus fulfilled Old Testament scriptures. He was as it were a new and greater Moses who delivered the new covenant instruction much as Moses had delivered the old. Luke, in the two volumes of Luke-Acts, was concerned to show how Jesus and then the Holy Spirit freed Christianity from the bonds of nationalistic Judaism to become a world faith. Jesus stood at the mid-point of history, fulfilling God's promises to Israel. After the resurrection and ascension the Spirit directed the Church from Jerusalem through Judaea and Samaria to the ends of the earth. Luke also was concerned, like all the Gospel writers, with special side issues: women, the poor, the Spirit, and prayer.

Each of these writings, then, had a theological slant which will not allow them to be read as a dispassionate and objective report on Jesus' life. In addition, each sought in different ways to present Jesus and the movement which began with him in the best light. All, for example, sought to shift the blame for Jesus' death from the Romans to the Jews. The reason for this is obvious. The Romans put Jesus to death as the possible leader of a revolution. They had no other interest in him. Christians had to explain how such a charge could have been made and to insist that Jesus' kingdom was not of this world. The answer was that the Jews distorted the case. Unfortunately, the Jewish people have suffered the effects of anti-Semitism ever since.

Do theological and historical biases such as these discredit the Gospels as sources for the life and ministry of Jesus altogether and thus render the "quest" impossible? This writer would say no. All sources, however objective they claim to be, have biases. They reflect the slanted viewpoints of their authors. At the same time most possess, in varying degrees, some element of fact. The fact that none of these is absolutely factual, however, does not take away all of their value. What it takes away is the dogmatic certainty with which historians in the past sometimes operated. With dogmatic certainty out of the question the historian speaks in terms of relative certainty. He approaches all sources critically and seeks to evaluate their accuracy from as many sides as possible. In the case of the Gospels one can safely conclude that a kernel of historical fact underlies the early Church's handling of the material. There is thus no justification for the skeptical attitude which would declare the whole story nothing but a figment of later Christian imagination. Behind the early Christian preaching, *kerygma*, lies an historical event, the man Jesus of Nazareth and his message.

The truth of the matter is, some things can be tested from sources besides the Gospels. The New Testament contains additional materials. In Paul's letters the historian will find certain facts about Jesus, some primitive traditions (for instance, concerning the Last Supper and the resurrection), a number of apparent quotations (Rom. 13:7, 10; Gal 5:14; 1 Cor. 7:10-12, 25:1 Thess. 4:15-17), and statements quoted by later writers as words of Jesus, albeit from Paul's letters. The Pauline and other speeches in Acts contain quotations of references to him. Acts also includes a report on the ascension. Hebrews 2:18, 4:15, and 12:3 and 1 Peter 2:12 make specific mention of Jesus. James manifests traces of the Lord's teaching.

Non-canonical Christian sources contain numerous sayings and occasional historical references. Although they add little to what can be reconstructed of his life and teachings from the canonical New Testament writings, they do supply an occasional tidbit which is of value. One has to remember here that, since the sayings of Jesus and stories about him circulated orally for many years before being written down, not all of these were collected and preserved in the canonical Gospels. Some independent stories and sayings, like the pericope of the woman taken in adultery which was inserted into the next of John's Gospel very early (7:53-8:11), have a ring of authenticity. If handled with caution, these can fill out the portrait which the canonical writings paint.

Besides Christian sources, the historian will find some factual information in non-Christian, both pagan and Jewish, sources. Although these provide little specific information, they prove beyond reasonable doubt that Jesus actually lived. Pagan references are found in a letter sent by Pliny, Governor of Bithynia, to the Emperor Trajan in A. D. 112; in the historian Tacitus, writing about A. D. 115 concerning Nero's persecution of Christians (A. D. 64-68); in Suetonius' *Life of Claudius* (A. D. 41-54), written about A. D. 120, and in his *Life of Nero*; two letters of the Emperor Hadrian, one to Minicius Fundunas, proconsul of Asia in 125, and one to the consul Servianus in 134; in a Syriac letter of a certain Marabar Serapion, who fled from Samosata when it was seized by Vespasian in A. D. 73; in a late second or early third century graffito inscribed on the wall of an ancient building at Rome, "Alexamenos worships his god," under the figure of a cross with a donkey's head; and in some witnesses quoted by Christian writers. The paucity of early references was due to the lack of impact which Christianity had on the cultured peoples of the Empire until the late second century. After A. D. 170 allusions abounded.

Jewish sources contain a few references, but they are of little value. Three passages in the *Antiquities* of the first century Jewish historian Josephus are of questionable authenticity. The *Talmud* contains some allusions which establish that the first century rabbis accepted Jesus as historical personage and held more temperate attitudes toward them. A curse against the "heretics," probably meaning Christians, was put in the Jewish liturgy around A. D. 85.

Finally, early archaeological evidence offers additional confirmation of the existence of Jesus, although it adds nothing to knowledge about him. By the mid-second century Christian catacomb art began to portray him. A third century church at Dura-Europos had a portrait also. Further, the name of Jesus appeared in formulas found at Pompeii and elsewhere dating from the first century.

The Pre-Galilean Ministry

Although the sources discussed above will not allow the historian to write a biography of Jesus, they will permit him to make some conjectures about the course of Jesus' brief life and ministry in the Palestinian context.

The Birth

Little can be said about the years before he began his public ministry in Galilee. Apart from the birth narratives in Matthew and Luke only one credible story has survived to fill the intermediate gap, the Lucan narrative of Jesus in the Temple at age twelve. Some fanciful later stories of creating birds out of clay and restoring a severed limb represent purely legendary inventions.

The birth and infancy narratives of Matthew and Luke supply more theological interpretation than historical fact. From them, however, it is possible to determine that Jesus was born before the death of Herod the Great in 4 B. C. Matthew's report that Herod sought to have all infants two years of age and under in Bethlehem and its environs put to death implies that Jesus may have been born as early as 6 B. C. The mention of Quirinus in Luke 2:2 creates a serious difficulty, however, for the established dates of his governorship were A. D. 6-11. A census was taken in A. D. 6 or 7, but none is known before the date given here. Quirinus may have been virtual governor of Syria in 3-2 B. C., but this is doubtful and would be too late for the birth of Jesus before the death of Herod in 4 B. C. There could have been a census, regularly taken every fourteen years, but this is doubtful.

A more precise birthdate cannot be established. December 25 was first suggested in the time of Constantine, evidently in connection with the festival in honor of the Sun God. Prior to that Christians in the East observed January 6, but no basis can be given for this calculation.

Matthew and Luke both placed Jesus' birth in Bethlehem. Some scholars have questioned the accuracy of this location, because both were concerned to draw out the messianic implications of the city. Bethlehem was commonly cited in Jewish sources as the birthplace of the Messiah. Bethlehem was David's city. Matthew saw the event as a fulfillment of Micah 5:1, 3. Luke went out of his way to connect this with the census.

Whatever one concludes about Jesus' birthplace, it is unlikely that the evangelists invented the picture of modest beginnings. Early tradition recorded Jesus' birth in a cave, which is not unlikely since caves often served as stables.

The visit of the Magi recorded by Matthew and that of the shepherds and angels recorded by Luke represent theological concerns of each evangelist. Later tradition numbered the Magi according to the number of gifts mentioned, but Matthew does not suggest as much. In Matthew's mind the three gifts probably symbolized Christ's offices — king (gold), priest (incense), and prophet (myrrh). In Luke the shepherds denoted God's visitation to deliver the lowly and oppressed among his people, a special concern of Luke.

As a son of pious Jewish parents, Jesus undoubtedly went through the traditional rites prescribed by the Law. Thus he received circumcision on the eighth day and was presented in the Temple, as required by Numbers 6:10. His "presentation" involved a dedication to God as the first-born son (1 Kings 1:24f.). His special recognition by the aged Simeon and Anna reflect once more Luke's special concerns. Simeon's blessing of the infant sounded a universalistic note based on Isaiah 40-66.

Debate waxes hot about the miraculous conception, that is, the so-called "virgin birth." A historian is not in a position to make a judgment concerning the accuracy of the reports in Matthew and Luke. It can be said on the positive side that neither of the evangelists seems to have introduced the account for a clearly discernible theological reason. Matthew reported rather matter-of-factly that "before they came together" Mary was "found to be with child of the Holy Spirit" (Matt. 1:18). Luke made somewhat more of the divine election of Mary as "the handmaiden of the Lord."

Jesus was the first child. Catholic tradition has maintained that Mary had no more children, instead remaining a virgin. This theory encounters difficulty with references in the Gospels to Jesus' brothers — James, Joses, Jude, and Simon (Mark 6:3; cf. Matt. 27:56). Since the time of Jerome, the explanation has been that they were not brothers but cousins, an explanation disputed by many. Since Joseph received no mention in Jesus' ministry, it would appear that he died while Jesus was young, thus leaving him to assist Mary in the rearing of her family (cf. Luke 4:22; John 6:42).

John the Baptist

The information about Jesus becomes more precise at the beginning of his public ministry. This ministry began in association with John the Baptist.

The significance of John the Baptist for Jesus' ministry is made clear by all four Gospels. At the outset Jesus may have contemplated becoming a follower of John. According to the Gospels, however, John himself dissuaded him. He should be the follower, not Jesus. He was a preparer of the way. He was pointing to someone, not himself, who would be the Messiah.

How accurate were the Gospels when they presented John in this way? It is necessary to give a cautious answer here, for modern scholarship has shown that the Gospel writers were engaged in a polemic against a John the Baptist sect which had a substantial following when they wrote. Luke referred directly to the sect in Acts 19:1ff. This sect evidently claimed that since John baptized Jesus, he was the greater of the two. They saw Jesus as a follower of John. Consequently it was in the interest of the evangelists to have John show deference to Jesus, to point to him as Messiah. They could have distorted the facts. Did they?

Careful study of the brief career of John the Baptist would indicate that he saw himself as a precursor of the Messiah. He was announcing and calling for action in view of the inbreak of the messianic age. His baptism was "a baptism of repentance for forgiveness of sins" in view of the crisis.

John's mission and message show many similarities with the self-understanding of the Qumran Covenanters. These similarities have led William H. Brownlee to propose that John, orphaned by the deaths of his aged parents in his early years, was reared by the Essenes. Among close parallels are a strong denunciation of Jewish society, especially priests, insistence upon baptism of all persons and not proselytes alone, and urgent stress upon judgment of fire. However, John differed from the Essenes at certain key points. His baptism was once-for-all and not self-administered, as were Essene ablutions. If John did once belong to the Qumran community, it is clear that, disappointed in the failure of the Essenes to implement Isaiah 40:3, he decided to appeal to the whole Jewish nation to repent. He thus went near the main arteries of traffic, in northern Judea, just below Galilee, to proclaim his message.

It is not likely that John thought of himself as the Messiah. By his references to fire he seems to have expected Elijah as the *type* of the Messiah, not the forerunner. John was proclaiming judgment to come — the cleaning of the threshing floor, the axe at the root of the tree, the wrath against a brood of vipers. Further, he was proclaiming the coming of one "mightier than I," a messianic judge, based on "the Son of Man" in Daniel 7.

Luke has dated the beginning of John's ministry "in the fifteenth year of the reign of Tiberius as Caesar." The phrase could mean either A. D. 28/29 or possibly 25/26, depending on whether one dates the reign from the death of Augustus (August 19, A. D. 14) or from Tiberius's co-reign with Augustus. His ministry did not last long, for he soon offended Herod Antipas and was cast into prison (Luke 3:19-20). Not long after, he was beheaded (Mark 6:17-29).

Jesus' Baptism

If Jesus once thought of himself as a follower of John, he soon went his own way. His baptism, about which there can be no question since it proved embarrassing to Christians to explain, was probably the point at which his own calling crystalized. What did his baptism signify?

Since John proclaimed "a baptism of repentance for forgiveness of sins" (Mark 1:4), Jesus' baptism undoubtedly represented a response to that message. Matthew was quick to have John point out, however, that the typical meaning did not fit Jesus himself. He would not have been responding on account of his own sense of sin.

Why, then, was he baptized? Matthew has quoted Jesus himself as saying, "Let it be so now; for thus it is fitting for us to fulfill all righteousness" (Matt. 3:15). The crucial word is the plural "us." Jesus was coming not on account of his personal consciousness of sin so much as on account of his identification with the people of Israel. John's preaching applied to the whole people. It called for the repentance of all together. So Jesus was responding on behalf of the people and not merely on behalf of himself.

The question is: Is this Jesus' or Matthew's interpretation? It could be Matthew's, for he alone has the statement. Further, early Christian theology quickly came to insist that Jesus did not share typical human sinfulness (Heb. 4:15). Nevertheless, if the words were Matthew's, they ring true with other things which can be discovered about Jesus' self-understanding. In particular, they agree with Jesus' understanding of himself as the Servant of God as implied by his chosen ministry.

The words of the voice from heaven which accompanied his baptism are quite revealing. All three of the Synoptic Gospels recorded this speech, although the Lucan version is somewhat different than Matthew's and Mark's. Luke was obviously correcting the quotation found in Mark and Matthew. The original quotation was a conflation of two Old Testament texts: Psalm 2:7 and Isaiah 42:1. The conflating of these two passages could have been made by the Church, but it is reasonable to believe that Jesus himself reported it in this way to an inner circle of disciples. The tendency of the Church would have been to make the kind of correction Luke made, quoting only Psalm 2:7.

If Jesus did relay to his disciples an interpretation of his experience such as the evangelists recorded, he left a clue to his understanding of his calling in the conflated scriptures. Psalm 2 was in ancient Israel an enthronement Psalm. By Jesus' day it was interpreted messianically. In citing Psalm 2:7, therefore, Jesus was interpreting himself as Messiah. Isaiah 42:1, however, was not a messianic passage but the first of four "Servant" poems in Deutero-Isaiah. If Jesus applied this to his understanding of his mission, he no doubt understood the latter in terms of Isaiah's Servant. He was a Servant Messiah, not a kingly Messiah after the model of David.

The correctness of this interpretation is confirmed by the temptation experiences which followed Jesus' baptism. These experiences may have been the creation of the evangelists or sources upon which they depended. All three of the Synoptists but especially Matthew and Luke present the temptation story in more or less mythological terms when it had to be a highly personal and interior experience. In the interest of presenting Jesus as the Messiah-Servant, they or their sources could have created the account. The forty days corresponded to the wilderness wanderings of Israel after the Exodus and escape through the Red Sea and to Moses' years in the wilderness. The temptation itself implies a connection between Jesus and Moses, Jesus and Elijah, etc.

Quite possibly, however, the account went back to Jesus himself. Why could he not have explained to an inner circle of his followers the interior experience which accompanied his calling? A period of fasting was not an uncommon way of responding in a time of stress and decision-making among the religious of his day. Further, Jesus himself could have employed the concrete mode of expression typical of prophets in describing an interior experience which went beyond words.

Whether Jesus' or the Church's interpretation, the import of the temptation story as presented by Matthew and Luke is clear. Jesus was rejecting the Messiah ben David role. He would not reduce his role to the satisfaction of material wants of the people, dramatic miracles, or military triumph. Others had tried those and failed. Instead, his way was to be the way of obedience to God and trust in his providence, that is, the way of the Servant.

A Judaean Ministry?

Jesus' baptism and finalizing of his call, therefore, inaugurated his ministry before he began preaching in Galilee. It is debated whether, as John recounts, he pursued a ministry in Judaea for a time before going to Galilee. For many years scholars tended to reject John's report, chapters 1-3, of the calling of some disciples, cleansing of the Temple, miracles, meeting with Nicodemus, and ministry parallel to John the Baptist's. In recent years this view has undergone some reassessment as a result of more careful studies in the fourth Gospel. Some scholars are at least willing to say that, while details are probably inaccurate, the possibility of a pre-Galilean ministry in Judaea has much in its favor. For one thing, the Synoptists as well as John imply a pre-Galilean ministry, probably as a time of preparation for a wider and more active ministry. Thus Mark, for example, on whom Matthew and Luke probably depended, reported that "after John was arrested, Jesus came into Galilee, . . . " (Mark 1:14).

The Galilean Ministry

Whatever may have happened prior to it, it was in his native Galilee that Jesus came to the notice of his countrymen. This ministry was in itself brief, thus not permitting the establishment of a chronology of events. What can be trusted in the evangelists' accounts is not the sequence of events. They supplied vignettes which would help to tell their readers who Jesus was and to evoke a response.

Because the next chapter will take up the teaching of Jesus in greater detail, it will suffice at this point to say that the heart of it was the Kingdom or Rule of God (*Malkuth Yah-weh*). He seems to have thought that the Rule of God was breaking into human history, the lives of the people of Israel, in and through his own ministry. He perhaps chose the term "Son of Man," although some scholars contend that Mark and not Jesus himself applied it to him, to embody his conviction that he, as Messiah-Servant, was signaling the inbreak of God's rule in a unique way. It is possible that Jesus' thought concerning the Kingdom of God underwent development. That was at least Mark's understanding. Early it seems to have focused on the Parousia of the Son of Man figure of Daniel 7. Later it turned toward the suffering and death of the Son of Man.

Healing the Sick

Not only Jesus' proclamation but his deliberate activity related closely to the inbreak of God's Kingdom in and through him. One important aspect of his ministry was healing of the sick. In the Galilean period the Gospels give a number of summary statements which suggest that healing was a typical activity. In addition, they related some direct examples: the curing of Peter's mother-in-law of a fever, the cleansing of the leper named Simon, and others.

A number of modern scholars have discounted the healing narratives and miracle stories, ascribing them to primitive mythology and early Christian embellishment. Some embellishment undoubtedly occurred. Moreover, the primitive world view and science of Jesus' day would have given a different cast to healings and other phenomena than the modern world view and science would.

At the same time healing as a part of Jesus' ministry cannot be dismissed lightly as primitive superstition. The Gospels contain too much material concerned with healing to allow that. Furthermore, healing claims were not confined to Jesus or the early Church. Jewish rabbis reported healings. And in the third century Philostratus recounted the feats of Apollonius of Tyana as the pagan counterpart to Jesus during the first century. In recent years, moreover, the modern scientific world view has undergone enough revision as to eliminate dogmatism. Healing is seen not merely as a physiological but much more as a psychosomatic process.

Discounting somewhat for embellishment, therefore, impressive evidence of Jesus' healing ministry remains. In the eyes of the evangelists the healing miracles were not wondrous feats to startle and make converts of unbelievers. Rather, they were "signs," as John called them, of the inbreaking of God's Kingdom in and through Jesus. According to Luke 4:16ff., Jesus inaugurated his ministry in his native city, Nazareth, by reading Isaiah 61:1, 2: "The Spirit of the Lord is upon me, because he has anointed me to preach good news to the poor. He has sent me to proclaim release to the captives and recovering of sight to the blind, to set at liberty those who are oppressed, to proclaim the acceptable year of the Lord." The words may represent Luke's interpretation: certainly they coincide with special interests of his. But they also echo the Servant motif which perhaps originated with Jesus himself.

Calling Disciples

In the early part of his ministry Jesus began to enlist disciples. At first perhaps he issued a rather general invitation, but as time went on he narrowed the circle to a more select group, the Twelve. Some scholars have argued that the number Twelve was an invention of the early Church, but, if so, it arose very, very early, for Paul knew of them as a part of tradition concerning the resurrection (1 Cor. 15:5). It seems more likely that the number originated with Jesus himself and reflected his messianic thinking. As Messiah-Servant, he was gathering around him a symbolic remnant. Whereas the twelve patriarchs and twelve tribes supplied the foundation of Israel under the old covenant, so the twelve apostles supplied the foundation of Israel under the new covenant.

Modern scholarship has shown that Jesus' calling differed

from that of contemporary teachers both in Judaism and in the Hellenistic world. In both of the latter it was customary for the pupil to seek out a teacher. Thus, typical of budding rabbis, Paul went to Jerusalem to study with Gamaliel II (Acts 22:3). Similarly, in the Hellenistic world, aspiring scholars went from school to school and teacher to teacher to get their education. Jesus, however, reversed the process. He sought out disciples. When he found one, he issued a command, the call of divine grace, to follow. Like his teaching, his call also reflected a unique sense of authority, bound up undoubtedly with his conviction that God's Kingdom was breaking into history in and through him.

As Eduard Schweizer has shown in *Lordship and Discipleship*, the call was, first of all, a call to allegiance to Jesus himself as the decisive act. The very wording indicated the intensity: "Here! Behind me!" (Mark 1:17). It involved, secondly, the beginning of something wholly new, that is, an act of divine grace. Following Jesus meant drinking "new wine," the wine of the Messianic age. It meant, thirdly, companionship with Jesus and service to him. Whatever the disciple did, it would be "for his sake" and "for the sake of the gospel." It entailed, fourthly, giving up all other ties. One who wanted to follow Jesus could not even return to pay his last respects to a deceased father (Matt. 8:21). Following meant renunciation of family. Whoever would forsake father, mother, sister, brother, children, or property for his sake would receive an eternal reward (Matt. 19:29; Mark 10:29-30; Luke 18:29b-30). Christ's real brethren are those who do the Father's will (Matt. 12:50; Mark 3:35; Luke 8:21). Finally, Jesus called disciples to share his rejection, suffering, and death, and through this to share his glory. Whoever would allow him would have to deny himself, take up his cross, and then follow. He would forfeit his life in order to get it back again (Mark 8:34).

The Sending of the Twelve

Jesus did not get a kind reception in his homeland. It is the unanimous testimony of the evangelists that his own people rejected him. Like the prophets, he was not held in esteem by his own people (Matt. 13:57; Mark 6:4; Luke 4:24; cf. John 1:11). Why? Part of the reason may have been a natural tendency to question claims of religious authority by a mere carpenter's son (Mark 6:3). Jesus was not an ordained rabbi, a recognized religious leader, but he spoke and acted with an authority which rabbis did not claim (Mark 1:22, 27). According to Luke, another part of the reason for rejection was related to Jesus' inaugural address in Nazareth. In the latter he had warned that Israel must not presume on God's election but should remember that God had shown favor towards others besides the Jews, the widow of Sidon and Naaman the Syrian (Luke 4:25-30). The incident may have been a Lucan reflection upon the outcome of Jesus' life and ministry, but it would not be difficult to believe that it occured early in Jesus' ministry. John the Baptist preached a similar message. God was playing no favorites in his demand of repentance.

Whatever the reason for rejection at Nazareth, it forced Jesus to expand his ministry to other parts of Galilee. The authority with which he taught and healed in Capernaum caused his reputation to spread throughout Galilee (Mark 1:28; Luke 4:37). As his reputation spread, his sense of urgency about the Galilean ministry increased. He had to proclaim the good news of the Kingdom. That was the reason God sent him.

As people came from everywhere to hear and be healed by this new prophet, Jesus gathered and commissioned the Twelve to extend his ministry of word and deed. The Twelve, whose names vary in the several lists found in the New Testament (Matt. 10:2-4; Mark 6:16-19; Luke 6:13-16; John 1:42; Acts 1:13), were sent, like Jesus (Matt. 15:24), to Jews only. The task was to obtain repentance in the house of Israel in order that the Kingdom might dawn. The disciples were to do as Jesus himself had done, and they received the same authority which he possessed.

Like Jesus' mission, the mission of the Twelve was also urgent. Jesus underlined the urgency by forbidding them to take bread, bag, and money. It is debated, however, whether Jesus believed that the Kingdom would be consummated in his own lifetime. On the basis of Matthew 10:23, "you will not have gone through all the towns of Israel, before the Son of man comes," Albert Schweitzer theorized that Jesus did expect that. When the expectation failed, he chose the Cross deliberately in an effort to force God to act. He, in Schweitzer's vivid imagery, threw himself on the wheel of the world, and it crushed him. Most New Testament scholars now disagree with Schweitzer's theory. The chief alternatives are to suppose that Jesus believed the Kingdom fully present in himself or inaugurated by him. The latter would appear to handle conflicting statements best. According to it, Jesus did conceive of the Kingdom as coming in and through his ministry but believed also that it would be consummated at some future date with the return of the heavenly Son of Man. The words of Matthew 10:23 represented a prophetic foreshortening.

The disciples' mission, therefore, ended in failure in the sense that the expected Consummation had not come. The failure doubtlessly caused Jesus to ponder more deeply than ever what his mission was. He was frustrated not so much by waning popularity as by a lack of repentance and belief in the immanence of the Kingdom of God. His frustration is reflected perhaps in the parable about the children playing in the market place and in his expression of woes over Chorazin and Bethsaida. Coupled with the fate of John the Baptist, his own reflection upon Isaiah 53 led him to a still deeper interpretation of the "Son of Man."

It has been proposed by T. W. Manson that this combination of events led to Jesus' withdrawal from public ministry. He did not withdraw because of fear of Herod (Luke 13:32ff). Rather, he was beginning to see that his ministry would have to take place in Jerusalem. But before that, he needed to prepare himself and his disciples.

The Withdrawal from Galilee

Most scholars consider the trip to Syria a watershed in Jesus' self-determination. This was the occasion for the formulation of the final outcome and aim of his ministry. At this point perhaps he connected his ministry with messianic suffering.

Jesus' withdrawal took him beyond the bounds of Israel. The story of his meeting with a Syro-Phoenician woman (Matt. 15:21-28; Mark 7:24-30) possibly reflects his own struggle with the limits of his ministry. Once again, as in sending out the Twelve, he asserted that his ministry was limited to "the lost sheep of the house of Israel." Such a restriction was natural, first, because he was himself a member of the Jewish nation, and, secondly, because he probably expected all nations to come together for the banquet of the end time after the conversion of Israel.

However this incident may have affected his ministry, the confession of Peter at Caesarea-Philippi seems to have finalized the Messiah-Servant concept. Some scholars have questioned the authenticity of the account, preferring to see it as an interpretation imposed later by the Church. Against this, however, others have argued that the Church, a community, could not create such an idea. The likely source would be Jesus himself.

If authentic, the incident tested once again Jesus' vocation. Who was he? His contemporaries interpreted him in various ways. Some saw him as John the Baptist returned to life, others as Elijah, and still others as some other prophet. In short, he was a prominent prophet, but not the Messiah. Peter, however, spokesman of the Twelve, more deeply initiated into the mystery of Jesus, was not content with the popular assessment. Jesus was the Messiah, the fulfiller of Israel's hopes.

Matthew has inserted at this point (Matt. 16:17-19) the famous and much-disputed passage about the "keys." Oscar Cullmann has suggested that, if it is authentic, it probably was not spoken at this time by Jesus. Perhaps it was a post-resurrection saying later transferred to this position.

According to the Marcan and Lucan accounts, Jesus charged the disciples not to disclose who he was. Then, he proceeded to issue the first of three predictions of his suffering and death. He was not to be the kind of Messiah the disciples expected but the Servant of Isaiah 53.

Did Jesus really predict his death? Some scholars have said no. They have preferred to see the passion sayings as reflections of the early Church from the vantage point of the cross. Others have argued to the contrary that Jesus could easily have foreseen his suffering and death as consequences of his ministry and especially of his claims of authority. Almost from the outset, in fact, he encountered conflict. Quite likely, the evangelists, looking backwards from the perspective of later experience, made his predictions more precise. This is evident, for example, in the way Matthew and Luke altered the Marcan statement that the Son of Man would be raised "after three days" to read "on the third day." The original statement meant "after a short time." Two later passion predictions (Mark 9:30-32; 10:32-34) increased in precision. This could have been due either to later Christian reflection or to the fact that Jesus gained more insight as he drew nearer to Jerusalem. It is not necessary, however, to suppose that later generations created the Servant motif.

The fact is, the disciples failed repeatedly to comprehend Jesus' understanding of messiahship. Peter's remonstrance represented once more the temptation which followed Jesus' baptism. At the time Judaism probably had no concept of a suffering Messiah.

The account of Jesus' transfiguration which followed the confession has been explained in several ways: (1) as a record of a factual experience, (2) as only a vision, (3) as a legend or symbolic story, a story after the event, (4) as purely symbolic, based on Jewish eschatological speculations, and (5) as a real experience but one about which no one can say precisely what happened. Whatever happened, the event deepened and confirmed the confession of messiahship. Moses and Elijah, representing the Law and the Prophets respectively, added their testimony. As at Jesus' baptism, the voice from heaven quoted messianic Psalm 2:7. The cloud which overshadowed him paralleled the cloud which hovered over the people at the Exodus, guiding and protecting them (Exod. 40:29). The point is, the disciples were illuminated and strengthened in their confidence in Jesus' messiahship.

The Jerusalem Ministry

In the course of the Galilean ministry, it would appear, Jesus came to the conclusion that his ministry could end only in Jerusalem. On what basis? In part, surely, because he recognized the importance of Jerusalem in the religion of Israel. Jerusalem was the capital. It was the center of Israel's faith and customs, both the Temple and the Law. In part also, Luke recounted, it was Jerusalem which put prophets to death. If it was his lot to die, it should be in Jerusalem, "for it cannot be that a prophet should perish away from Jerusalem" (Luke 13:33).

As is true of Jesus' entire ministry, it is not possible to establish a chronology for the journey to Jerusalem and ministry there. Maurice Goguel has proposed, on the basis of references in the Gospel of John, that Jesus left Galilee before the Feast of Tabernacles (John 7:2) in September/October, taught at Jerusalem until the Feast of Dedication (John 10:22) in December, and soon after retired beyond the Jordan River to Perea. Mark, however, telescoped the entire ministry into a six-day period.

Jesus probably followed the "pilgrim way" to Jerusalem with a number of interruptions. Mark related that he went through Capernaum, Samaria, and Jericho. To pass through Samaria and Jericho meant that he took the only road which crossed from East to West over the Jordan valley to a point above twelve miles above the Dead Sea to Bethany beyond the Jordan in Perea. On the way he continued his public ministry but sought in the main to instruct the disciples concerning his mission. Increasingly, he prepared them to reckon with the death of their leader.

According to the evangelists, the Jerusalem ministry began with the so-called "triumphal entry." The event has been interpreted by some scholars as a "messianic legend" or a product of the "messianic secret" of Mark. It has been interpreted by others as an actual happening. If the latter, it may have been either a messianic symbol, a spontaneous outburst of pilgrims and followers which was later interpreted messianically, or an event which was messianic for Jesus but not for the people generally. Clearly it was a prophetic act, an acted parable, teaching the nature of Jesus' mission as Servant. Jesus was fulfilling the Zechariah passage concerning a humble Messiah.

The Jerusalem ministry brought Jesus into conflict with the established authorities in a new way. Earlier, in Galilee, he seems to have been criticized by them for laxity in regard to the observance of the Law. He had earned the reputation of a playboy, friend of tax collectors and sinners (Matt. 11:19; Luke 7:34). He allowed his disciples to violate ritual rules concerning cleanliness, the sabbath, and other things. Then he had responded that rules were made to help rather than burden human beings. He had directed his ministry at outcasts in Jewish society and contended that it was the sick who needed a doctor.

The cleansing of the Temple, which probably came early in the Jerusalem ministry, probably precipitated the final controversy over authority. Jesus' action, as Vincent Taylor has said, represented "a spirited protest against injustice and the abuse of the Temple system." It was not an attack on the sacrificial system as such. Rather, it was both a prophetic and a messianic act. It was believed that the Temple would be purified in the messianic age. The cursing of the fig tree (Mark 11:15-19), if historical, may have been an acted parable concerning the fate of Israel and the Temple.

In his ministry, and especially in the cleansing of the Temple, Jesus was seen challenging the twin pillars of Judaism. On his own authority he claimed to stand above the Law and above the Temple. The query of priests, scribes, and elders, therefore, came as no surprise: "By what authority are you doing these things? Or who gave you the authority to do these things?" (Mark 11:28). According to the evangelists, Jesus avoided a direct reply. Like the rabbis, he put them on the horns of a dilemma by asking a counter-question: "By what authority did John the Baptist do what he did?" John was popular, widely regarded as a prophet, a man of God. The antagonists could not admit this without admitting also that Jesus, to whom John bore witness, was also a rabbi instructed by God. They chose to confess ignorance.

Jesus responded further with a series of parables. His parables were, as modern studies have proven, polemical as well as hortatory instruments. The parables of the lost sheep, the lost coin, and the prodigal son (Luke 15), for instance, defended his ministry to the outcasts. In their essential point they declared, "God cares for the lost." Similar in import were the parable of the two sons (Matt. 21: 28-32) and of the wicked husbandman (Matt. 21:33-46; Mark 12:1-12; 20:9-19) which the evangelists placed in the Jerusalem period.

A number of Jesus' parables warned about the imminence of catastrophe. Jesus was announcing the coming judgment, sounding an alarm, and calling for repentance in view of the imminent crisis. Like children in the market-place, his contemporaries played while Rome burned (Matt. 11:16-19; Luke 7:31-35). They had clear signs but failed to observe them (Matt. 16:2-3; Luke 12:54-56). The Son of Man would come like a thief in the night (Matt. 24:37-41; Luke 17:28ff.). None should be caught like the rich fool (Luke 12:13-21). They should take a lesson from the faithful and wise steward (Matt. 24:45-51; Luke 12:42-46). They should put their money to good use while time permitted, before the master returned for an accounting (Matt. 25:14-30; Luke 19:12-27). They must be vigilant and faithful like the doorkeeper (Matt.

24:43-51; Luke 12:35-38). They must not build on sand but on a rock (Matt. 7:24-27; 6:47-49).

According to Matthew and Mark, Jesus wept over the unrepentant city. He wished to draw it under his wing as a hen draws her brood, but Jerusalem did not respond (Matt. 23:37-39; Luke 13:34-35). Scholars have debated sharply the authenticity of the Marcan "little apocalypse" (Mark 13) and parallels in Matthew and Luke. Did Jesus predict the fall of Jerusalem or did the Church read that into his thought? What did he say about the end?

Scholars are widely agreed that Mark 13 is composite, consisting of both Jesus' own words and those of the early Church. They note also that doctrinal and catechetical materials of a later time have become embedded in the material used by Mark. Nevertheless, Mark 13 does contain some genuine sayings of Jesus adapted to later conditions. Considering the rather general nature of the sayings about the fall of Jerusalem, it is not difficult to believe that Jesus might have predicted it. At the same time Jesus may have used the occasion to warn his disciples again about seeing in that event the eschatological consummation. Indeed, it is difficult to avoid the conclusion that Jesus expected the return of the Son of Man and the consummation to occur within his own lifetime (Mark 13:30). His "error" was due to prophetic foreshortening. So urgent was his sense of mission, it seemed as if God had to consummate his kingdom immediately.

Was this a change in Jesus' thinking? Some scholars have suggested that it was. In the earlier phase of his ministry he may have taught what C. H. Dodd has called "realized eschatology," that is, he stressed the Kingdom of God in its present aspects. By the time he reached Jerusalem, however, he may have shifted to the future tense. He majored on the fate of Jerusalem, the eschatological aspect of the kingdom, and his return. That he taught his own return seems to be implied in the parables of the thief at midnight, the waiting servants, the talents, and the ten virgins.

The response which Jesus received in Jerusalem, especially from the masses, prompted him to withdraw beyond the Jordan. According to Johannine chronology, the withdrawal would have followed the Feast of Tabernacles and lasted until the following Passover in March/April. The withdrawal was prompted not by his enemies, the religious leaders, but by his friends. They could not comprehend the nature of his calling. They saw in him a leader, a messiah, but not a suffering one. They wanted to enthrone him like David (John 6:50).

Jesus withdrew also to ponder further the secret of messianic suffering and death. He withdrew to prepare himself for the final act of surrender. On the cross he alone would represent the people of God.

5

The Teaching of Jesus

The same scholars who question whether one can determine anything about the life and ministry of Jesus also question whether one can pick out his teaching from the midst of the early Church's teaching. Comparative study of his parables and other sayings in Gospel parallels turns up evidence of embellishment, changes of audience, hortatory use by the Church, influences of the Church's situation, and allegorization. Form critics have pointed out that this process of modification preceded the written documents. Indeed, Jesus' sayings circulated as independent pericopae over a thirty to fifty year period before being collected, the churches still expecting his return. A delay of Christ's return, or *Parousia*, finally forced the writing down of his words but not before they had undergone considerable reshaping. What was written down, therefore, represented the mind of the early Church much more than the mind of Jesus himself. When sifted, it leaves little that one can confidently attribute to Jesus himself.

This highly skeptical attitude toward the sources has been disputed by other scholars. Some have pointed out that, by virtue of the way Jesus taught in an oriental setting, many of Jesus' sayings survived with little or no alteration. His sayings give evidence of accurate preservation, for example, in Aramaisms, which, while not offering irrefutable proof that the words came from Jesus himself, tend to favor at least a Palestinian origin. Furthermore, much of Jesus' teaching was delivered in memorable forms, such as poetry, parables, and aphorisms, so as to be easily remembered. Orientals learned by rote memorization, and Jesus' sayings could easily become fixed in the minds of his hearers. Indeed, T. W. Manson contended in his study of *The Teaching of Jesus* that Jesus' sayings betray signs of delivery to different audiences — the masses, the religious leaders, and an inner circle of disciples. The last named group would have received and conserved much of his instruction and handed it down to others with care. The fact that some alteration has occurred by later times, therefore, should not undermine confidence that the early believers preserved a credible core of Jesus' own words.

This chapter is written in the assumption that the second position is more accurate than the first. It presupposes that, while dogmatic certainty is unattainable, some of the main lines of Jesus' thought can be determined even now. Early Christianity surely did not depart from these lines precipitously, for already by the time of Paul the words of Jesus had been elevated to the level of scripture. Paul, for instance, decisively distinguished between his word and the "word of the Lord" in answering Corinthian questions about divorce (1 Cor. 7:10, 12). The Lord's word held an authority which Paul's did not.

Jesus' Teaching Style

Before examining the content of Jesus' teaching, it will be useful to look briefly at its language and form.

Jesus' language was probably Aramaic, the vernacular of Palestine. He may have known some Greek but would probably not have taught in it. It is entirely possible that he knew and used rabbinic Hebrew, the language of learned debate. Such a conjecture is sustained by several bits of data: First, he quoted the Old Testament and read from it. Second, his own disciples and members of the public, even the learned, ad-

dressed him as rabbi (Mark 12:14, 32). Third, he was reported to have taught in the synagogues during the early part of
his ministry. Fourth, his ability at age twelve indicates that
he would probably have pursued study of this sort. Finally,
his humble origin would not have hindered his education.

The two most characteristic features of Jesus' teaching
were poetry and parable. His poetry manifests all three of the
characteristics of Hebrew poetry. The most distinctive characteristic was the use of parallel lines either synonymous with
one another, antithetical to one another, or these two combined. To these types, however, Jesus added a fourth, which
C. F. Burney called "step-parallelism." In this type the second
line picks up the thought of the first and develops the thought
further. Mark 9:37 supplies a good example:

"Whoever receives one such child in my name receives
me; and whoever receives me, receives not me but him
who sent me."

The other two characteristics of Hebrew poetry involved
parallelism also, in this case parallelism of sound as well as
sense. One was rhythm, which depends upon the number of
stressed syllables to a line. A third was rhyme. To find them
in Jesus' poetry almost requires retranslation.

The most striking feature of Jesus' teaching was his use of
parables. As a matter of fact, the extent of his use of parables
was unprecedented in Judaism. For the entire Old Testament
scholars have found only a handful. Further examples
appeared in rabbinic literature but not with the frequency
with which they turned up in Jesus' teaching. The rabbinic
examples were closer in form to Jesus' parables than the Old
Testament examples. Some were short, pithy, proverbial
statements; others were developed forms of illustration or allegory. In addition, the rabbis used a similar formula to in-
troduce their parables. Altogether, the canonical Gospels
contain sixty-five parables.

Such extensive usage implies special purpose. What this
purpose was has always been obscured by debate over the

explanation of the reason for parables in Mark 4:11-12 and parallels: "To you has been given the secret of the kingdom of God, but for those outside everything is in parables; so that they may indeed see but not perceive, and may indeed hear but not understand; lest they should turn again, and be forgiven." Taken at face value, this statement suggests that parables were used to confound outsiders. The results would seem to belie such a purpose, however. The hearers understood very well, for example, the parables about the widow of Sidon and Namaan the Syrian in Luke 4:25-30.

The solution to this problem probably lies in a proper understanding of Hebrew use of paradox. Although the purpose of a particular parable may have varied according to context, the object was to awaken a response of faith and repentance. A parable thus became a test of those who wanted to be disciples, or, in controversy with opponents, defended Jesus and his ministry. Often it resulted in rejection.

As vexing as the question of purpose is, it is exceeded by that of interpretation. From a very early date the parables were interpreted allegorically, that is, with particulars applied to a reader's situation without regard to the original meaning of the parable itself. The use of this method was no doubt reinforced by the fact that the Synoptic Gospels incorporated an allegorical interpretation of the parable of the sower, ostensibly by Jesus himself (Matt. 13:18-23; Mark 4:13-20; Luke 8:11-15). That this interpretation probably did not originate with Jesus himself is proven by the un-Hebraic character of the style, the vocabulary, the impression conveyed by the parable that a Christian community already existed, and the allegorical emphasis upon details. That such a thing could happen is explained by the way in which Jesus' words were conserved in early Christianity. A sermon cited Jesus' words and then added the preacher's interpretation. Later, on, both the parable and the interpretation circulated as Jesus' own saying.

Proper interpretation of the parables of Jesus requires attention to several points. First of all, in most cases a parable will have a single point, exceptions being double-edged parables like the parable of the prodigal son. Individual details should therefore be interpreted as necessary to the whole, but analogies to the details should not be asserted. Second, the context in which the parable appears will usually be that of the evangelists and influenced by them. Third, there will be evidence both of the life situation of the early Church and of Jesus himself. Finally, one must take care to discern embellishments which betray later application. When these factors are taken into account, the parables will offer the most trustworthy guidance to Jesus' own teaching which one can find.

God as Father

It has become virtually a truism to say that Jesus' chief message concerned the kingdom or rule of God. It has also been generally accepted that he believed the kingdom was being realized in and through his ministry. His works bore witness to the presence of the kingdom. His reply to John the Baptist's query as to whether he was the expected Messiah was: "Go and tell John what you hear and see: the blind receive their sight and the lame walk, lepers are cleansed and the deaf hear, and the dead are raised up, and the poor have good news preached to them" (Matt. 11:4-5; cf. Luke 7:22). Similarly, his response to scribes (Mark 3:22) or Pharisees (Mark 12:24) who charged that he expelled demons by Satanic power was that no Kingdom which is divided against itself can stand. "But if it is by the Spirit of God that I cast out demons, then the kingdom of God has come upon you" (Matt. 12:28; cf. Luke 11:20). His deeds spoke for him!

In the minds of religious leaders this claim represented a blasphemous assertion of authority. So did his teaching. The people noticed that "he taught them as one who had authority, and not as the scribes" (Mark 1:22; Matt. 7:29; cf. Luke 4:32). He used the typical rabbinic method of arguing, "You have heard that it was said...," but he was unique in the authoritative, "But I say..." He did not hesitate to challenge not merely his contemporaries' interpretations but even Moses' legislation. Moses allowed divorce "for your hardness of heart," "but from the beginning it was not so. *And I say to you:* whoever divorces his wife, except for unchastity, and marries another, commits adultery" (Matt. 19:8). He claimed authority not only to heal and to teach but even to forgive sins, a prerogative reserved to God alone (Mark 2:7). According to the evangelists, he substantiated this authority by healing a paralytic (Mark 2:1-12; Matt. 9:1-8; Luke 5:17-26). Finally, the cleansing of the Temple represented a final assertion of authority to speak or act in God's behalf.

What was the source of Jesus' claims of authority, which no amount of critical examination can explain away? Obviously it was not the authority of an ordained rabbi. Some of his contemporaries called him "rabbi," but they knew him also as a carpenter or carpenter's son. And those who held rabbinic credentials disputed his authority to do what he was doing. He lacked the proper credentials.

The source of his claims could have been a "prophetic consciousness." In his own mind he was a prophet (Mark 6:4; Matt. 13:57). He spoke and acted enough like a prophet for many of his contemporaries to recognize him as another John the Baptist, Elijah, or some other prophet (Mark 6:15; 8:28; Matt. 21:11, 46; Luke 7:16, 39; 9:8; 19; 24:19), or as "the prophet" spoken of by Moses (John 1:21). Prophets acted and spoke, as Jesus did, with the authority of God's word.

At this point the Christian has to ask a very hard question: "If prophetic consciousness was the source of Jesus' claims to authority, did the early Church err when it went further to ascribe a 'divine consciousness' as related to his messiahship? Did it do that solely on the basis of the resurrection experience and not at all on the basis of Jesus' own self-understanding and teaching?"

From an early date some have answered both questions in the affirmative. Jesus himself had no consciousness of "divinity." He spoke and acted just as did any other inspired prophet. He had no unique self-consciousness. He was proclaiming the kingdom of God in prophetic fashion. His claims went no further. Indeed, he himself disclaimed a suggestion that he was on a level with God himself. Of the rich young man who called him "good" teacher, he asked, "Why do you call me good? No one is good but God alone" (Mark 10:18).

Objective study shows, therefore, that early Christianity read much of its own faith into Jesus' self-understanding. Among the evangelists Mark alone exercised restraint in having followers identify Jesus as "the Son of God" in the sense of divine consciousness. Even in Mark Peter could confess openly at Caesarea-Philippi that Jesus was "the Christ (Messiah), the Son of the living God" (Matt. 16:16). Though such a confession would not imply consciousness of divinity in the Greek sense, it might imply more about messianic consciousness than Jesus himself intended.

When full allowance has been made for the early Church's backward look, however, it is still necessary to concede that Jesus' self-understanding possessed a uniquely authoritative character. This uniqueness is reflected, above all, in his confession of and prayer to God as Father. That such thinking went back to Jesus and not just the early Church is demonstrated by several things.

One, possibly the most basic, evidence for his unique sense of sonship is his use of an intimate personal address for God, "Abba" (Mark 14:36). Although God was occasionally addressed as "Our Father" in the Old Testament and in Judaism, he was never addressed in the way Jesus normally addressed him, as "my Father" or simply as "Father." The Aramaic word Abba corresponded to the American word "daddy." It reflected Jesus' unique filial consciousness, one that transcended prophetic consciousness.

T. W. Manson has pointed out that, in Jesus' own usage, addressing God as "father" was not commonplace. The fact that the evangelists used it so often means that they drew the conclusion that this concept stood at the center of his thinking. God was for him the supreme personal reality in the universe. Jesus, therefore, did not have to speak as scribes and Pharisees nor even as a prophet, "Thus saith the Lord..." He could say, rather, "I say unto you" because of his unique experience of sonship.

The intimacy of Jesus' filial relationship may be reflected in a statement in Matthew 11:27 and Luke 10:22 whose authenticity was once seriously questioned but now frequently affirmed by scholars: "All things have been delivered to me by my Father; and no one knows who the Son is except the Father, or who the Father is except the Son and any one to whom the Son chooses to reveal him" (Luke 10:22). For obvious reasons this statement has been labeled "the Johannine bolt from the blue." As a statement made to an inner circle of disciples it is more credible than it would have been as a statement to the public. It is not beyond belief that Jesus may have let his consciousness of being God's special instrument of revelation shine through.

A similar consciousness peeks through the parable of the wicked husbandmen (Matt. 21:33-46; Mark 12:1-12; Luke 20:9-19), unanimously assigned by the evangelists to the Jerusalem period. The owner of a vineyard entrusted his vineyard to tenant farmers. When he sent his servants (the prophets?) for an accounting, the tenants beat and then killed them. Finally, he sent his "beloved son," but they killed him too. As it now stands in the Gospels, the parable has undergone allegorization. In its original form, however, it doubtless defended Jesus' mission to the poor and rejected of Jewish society against criticisms of religious leaders. Quite possibly, Jesus envisioned himself as the son sent to do what prophets failed to do but also failing.

The teaching of Jesus about God's fatherhood reflected deep personal experience, an experience of intimate communion in prayer. The Church has traditionally believed that Jesus summarized his teaching in the so-called "Lord's Prayer" or "Our Father." Although its original form is not certain, its present Matthaean form gives two themes. First, God as Father is the sovereign arbiter of world history. Second, he cares for and ministers to each child. Authentic faith is, above all, faith in his providence which is so intimate as to include the common field lilies, the sparrows, and the hairs of human heads. It is the faith of the trusting child who does not doubt the Father's care.

The Kingdom of God

This understanding of God as Father carries over into Jesus' teaching concerning the kingdom of God. Unfortunately no teaching of Jesus, central as it was to his thinking, has been subject to more misinterpretation, in opposite directions. On the one hand, some have idealized the present, for example, a "Christian America." On the other hand, others have looked only for "pie in the sky by and by."

In Jesus' thought the kingdom of God was, first of all, a relationship which God, not men, would establish. Jesus' parables offered assurance that the kingdom would come without human intervention — like seed, which grows "of itself" (Mark 4:26-29), like mustard seed, which becomes great despite insignificant beginnings as though by some miraculous power (Mark 4:30-32; Matt. 13:31-32; Luke 13:18-19), or like leaven, which acts mysteriously (Matt. 13:33; Luke 13:20-21). Human beings, Jewish revolutionaries included, could not "force" God to establish his rule. God first manifests his rule in the life of the individual, then He extends it to society.

This understanding of the kingdom or rule of God, as T. W. Manson has remarked, makes the question as to whether the kingdom is present or future irrelevant. When the rule of God is accepted, it becomes a present reality to the subject. It increases until the final consummation with the coming of the

Son of Man, a future event. Thus it is eternal, both present and future at the same time. In Jesus' teaching the kingdom was a present reality as something which was coming into existence in and through his own ministry, but it was also future, awaiting the "coming of the Son of man" (Mark 13:26, 32; 14:62) "the day" (Mark 13:32) or the "Parousia" (Matt. 24:3, 27, 37, 39). All three aspects of the kingdom — God's sovereignty, present reality, future hope — belonged not only to Jesus' teaching but also to the Old Testament, rabbinic Judaism, and primitive Christianity.

Jesus' deeds and words proclaimed that the day of salvation was at hand. The kingdom was present in restoration of sight to the blind, in recovery of physical faculties by the lame, in the cleansing of lepers, in the opening of deaf ears, in raising the dead, and in preaching to the poor (Luke 7:22; Matt. 11:5). All incidents of healing were, in Jesus' mind, indications, acted parables, as it were, that the messianic era had dawned.

Parables called attention to this same point. Jesus' disciples did not have to fast like those of John or the Pharisees, for wedding guests do not fast while the bridegroom is still with them (Mark 2:19). Similarly, one does not put a new patch on an old garment or new wine in old wineskins, for the new will split the old (Mark 2:21-22). One could tell by signs that the time was at hand in the way a farmer could tell when figs were ready for picking (Mark 13:28-29).

The immanence of the kingdom in Jesus not only assured his hearers of salvation, however. It also announced the imminence of catastrophe, God's judgment, and sounded a call for repentance. Despite the signs of the times (Matt. 16:2-3; Luke 12:54-56), Jesus' contemporaries played like children (Matt. 11:16-19; Luke 7:31-35). The day of the Son of Man would come suddenly, unexpectedly, as the flood of Noah's day (Matt. 24:37-41; Luke 17:28ff.). The situation should caution all against acting like the rich fool who went on building barns for tomorrow and lost his life during the night (Luke 12:13-21). Each must respond with dispatch in light of the crisis, being as it were a careful steward of his talents (Matt. 25:14-30; Luke 19:12-27), watchful and faithful (Matt. 24:43-51; Luke 12:35-38), imitating the faithful and wise servant (Matt. 24:45-51; Luke 12:42-46), building on a rock (Matt. 7:24-27; Luke 6:47-49).

Jesus not only announced the crisis; he urged his hearers to respond immediately. They should act wisely like the debtor who sought to settle accounts before taken into court (Matt. 5:25-26; Luke 12:57-59). Like the rich man in the Dives-Lazarus parable, they might not have a second chance to repent and reform (Luke 16:19-31). How dreadful to be caught like the man who came to the wedding feast of the king without a wedding garment (Matt. 2:11-13) or the five foolish maidens who did not bring enough oil for their lamps (Matt. 25:1-13). Each person who would enter the kingdom should count the cost, like the tower builder or the king going to war (Luke 14:28-32). He should make proper preparation and set his own house in order. If he failed to do a thorough housecleaning, he would find a whole house full of evil spirits taking the place of one expelled (Matt. 12:43-45; Luke 11:24-26). To enter the kingdom would involve renouncing self-righteous pretensions and abasing oneself before God, as it were, choosing the lower place at the banquet table (Luke 14:7-11), and becoming a little child, that is, learning dependence upon God (Matt. 18:2-3; Mark 9:36; 10:15; Luke 9:48; 18:17).

The most heatedly disputed implication of Jesus' ministry and message was that through him God was expressing mercy and forgiveness toward sinners. Jesus responded to attacks with parables which depicted God's love for the sinner. The three parables of Luke 15 — the lost sheep, the lost coin, and the prodigal son — forcefully reminded his detractors that God has more concern for the lost than for those who are secure. Heaven rejoices more over the return of one lost sheep, the recovery of one lost coin, or the return of one prodigal than over ninety-nine sheep in the fold, a handful of coins in the bank, or the faithful elder brother.

Jesus' critics found this contention both perplexing and irritating. Should not they, like the elder brother of Jesus' parable, receive more from God? Jesus responded negatively. Like the kind employer who gave each laborer the same reward, no matter how long his labor, God rewards not on the basis of merit but by grace (Matt. 20:1-16). The one essential element in the justification of any person is his repentance and trust in God. The problem of the "self-righteous" lies here. They tend to have confidence in themselves rather than in God, like the Pharisee who thanked God that he was so devout. In self-righteousness, they alienate themselves from God.

Jesus believed that the position of the sinner who knew his sinfulness was better than the position of the good person who did not acknowledge sin. The sinner might beat his breast in genuine repentance and trust in the heavenly Father, and the Father would forgive him, no matter if he were an undeserving tax-collector (Luke 18:9-14). Surely God would hear the plea of one who begged for mercy more quickly than an evil judge would respond to the plea of a poor woman in need (Luke 18:2-8a). Indeed, he acts more readily to grant the petition of those who ask than the friend who will get up at midnight to give a loaf of bread (Luke 11:5-8) or the human father whose son begs for food (Matt. 7:7-11; Luke 11:9-13). From the human side, the one who receives the greater forgiveness will respond with greater love (Luke 7:41ff.). What matters is not how long one has shown faithfulness but whether one has done so with his whole heart, soul, and strength. Better to be the son who said he would not do the Father's bidding, then repented and did it, than to be the son who said he would do it and then did not (Matt. 21:28-32).

Discipleship in the Kingdom

What Jesus envisioned, then, was the inbreaking of a new era in the relationship between God and his people. Although both the idea of God as Father and that of God as King had ample precedent in the Old Testament, Jesus' belief that the eschatological age was dawning in and through his ministry introduced a quite different perspective in the relationship between God and man and between man and man. The era of the new covenant would differ from that of the old covenant.

Much of Jesus' teaching concerning discipleship is summarized in the Sermon on the Mount. In its present form the Sermon cannot be viewed as a sermon or address delivered by Jesus on a single occasion. It represents, rather, a collection of sayings compiled by Matthew as a summary of Jesus' teaching concerning the righteousness expected of those who belong to the kingdom. The kingdom demands a righteousness which goes beyond that of scribes and Pharisees (Matt. 5:20). It demands that a disciple be "perfect" (Matt. 5:48) or "merciful" (Luke 6:36) even as God is "perfect" or "merciful." In short, the ethic of the kingdom is absolute.

This is a difficult saying. Indeed, it is so difficult that Christian scholars have sought various paths around it. One has been to *spiritualize* it by saying that Jesus did not mean any of his sayings to be applied literally. Another has been to say that Jesus meant to apply its provisions to the *future kingdom* and not to the present. A third has been to stress the *paradoxes* in it which would allow the disciple to adjust his life-style to the present ambiguities. In the end none of these routes proves faithful to the sermon itself. This writer concurs with A. M. Hunter in viewing it as "an *unattainable* ethic which, as Christians, we must nevertheless try to attain."

However one resolves such critical questions, it is surely correct to say that Jesus' ethical teaching rested upon two great pillars — love of God and love of neighbor (Mark 12:29-31). Neither of these originated with Jesus himself. The first commandment was the Jewish Shema (Deut. 6:4-5), the second was a quotation of Leviticus 19:18. The originality of Jesus lay in a universalizing of the love commandment. Thus, whereas in Judaism "Love your neighbor" meant "Love your fellow Israelite" and even "Hate the stranger or non-Jew,"

Jesus taught, "Love your enemies" (Matt. 5:44). Disinterested, universal love would identify one as a son of the heavenly Father who lets his sun shine and his rain fall without partiality. Tax collectors and Gentiles return the love of their friends. A son of God must love as God loves. That is his "perfection" (Matt. 5:43-48).

The love ethic employs a different motive for behavior. The motive is not external but internal, an experience of God's boundless love and forgiveness, an experience of sonship. Righteousness before God depends not upon tithing mint, dill, and cummin, ritual cleansing of utensils, keeping sabbath regulations, whitewashing tombs, and observing other minutiae of the law. Rather, it depends upon the inner person, upon the heart. From an evil heart will come evil thoughts and deeds. From a good heart will come good thoughts and deeds (cf. Mark 7:14, 21-22; Matt. 15:11). The happy, the fortunate, therefore, are those whose hearts God has put right. The kingdom of God, the beatitudes say, belongs to those who depend utterly upon God for their righteousness. They are the ones whose righteousness can surpass that of the scribes and Pharisees.

The claim that a cleansed heart would go beyond the righteousness of scribes and Pharisees is striking, for no religious group ever acted with greater compunction to do the law. This claim, however, lay at the center of Christ's critique of Pharisaism. In imposing the law of love, Jesus would not "destroy" the old covenant law but "fulfill" it (Matt. 5:17). In what sense "fulfill"? Some scholars have viewed this statement as an interpolation of Matthew and not a word of Jesus. Such a conclusion is possible in light of the fact that the Apostle Paul declared Christ to be "the end of the law" in the sense that justification depends upon faith alone (Rom. 10:4). It is permissible, however, to interpret these words in other ways. By his ministry and teaching Jesus carried the law and the prophets to their proper conclusion by adding something. In other words, he completed them. Further, he brought out

their true meaning. By adhering to the commandment of love
the disciple "fulfills" the law. Put in Paul's words, all of the
commandments "are summed up in this sentence, 'You shall
love your neighbor as yourself'" (Rom. 13:8-10).

Several examples illustrate how the love ethic would carry
a disciple beyond the letter of the Old Testament and of the
religious teachers of Jesus' day. Whereas they taught, "Don't
kill," Jesus taught, "Don't be angry or insult your brother.
Instead, seek reconciliation" (Matt. 5:21-26). Whereas they
taught, "Don't commit adultery," Jesus taught, "Remove the
source of adultery, the inner desire which leads astray"
(Matt. 5: 27-30). Whereas they insisted on protecting the
wife's interest by a legal document of divorce, Jesus forbade
divorce altogether on the grounds that it forced the wife into
adultery (Matt 5:31-32). Here the exception clause was
almost certainly introduced by Matthew, for it appeared in
none of the other New Testament references to Jesus'
teaching on divorce (cf. Matt. 19:9; Mark 10:11-21; Luke
16:18; 1 Cor. 7:10f). Whereas the Old Testament and
religious leaders condoned oathtaking, Jesus urged that the
disciples make his word his bond (Matt. 5:33-37). Whereas
they encouraged exact retaliation, he encouraged non-resis-
tance, reconciliation, and giving without expectation of return (Matt. 5:33-42).

The distinction between these two ethical approaches is
very evident, but the way in which it should be characterized
is less so. An outstanding feature is the *interior motive* for
behavior. People, like trees, are known by their fruits. "A
sound tree cannot bear evil fruit, nor can a bad tree bear
good fruit" (Matt. 5:18; cf. Luke 6:43). This inward purity,
which God effects in the inner life of one who surrenders to
his rule, produces an appropriate response to specific situations. It will not allow the disciple to sidestep responsibility
by citing a rule. Made righteous by God, for example, one
could not use the Corban rule to escape an obligation to his
parents. This rule allowed a son to declare money or possessions which might aid his parents a "gift" to God and thus

avoid using these to meet the parents' needs. Under God's rule the disciple would take advantage of no casuistry to escape a responsibility.

Jesus aimed the main thrust of his critique of scribal and Pharisaic approaches to religion directly at this kind of casuistry. Their minute rules and regulations for religious observance got in the way of obedience to the will of God which they were designed to assist people in achieving. Sabbath regulations, for example, forbade healing anyone on the sabbath except in a life-or-death situation. Such rules, Jesus maintained, interfered with doing a good which was clearly in accordance with God's will. "The sabbath was made for man, not man for the sabbath" (Mark 2:27). He took a similar view of rules concerning cleanness and uncleanness (Mark 7:1-24). It was the intolerable assertion of authority which such judgments implied that set the religious leaders in inflexible opposition to him. As they viewed this, he was placing himself above the law (cf. Mark 3:6).

What Jesus sought in religion, perhaps from the backdrop of Jeremiah's new covenant concept (Jer. 31:31), was radical, totally sincere faith — love of God with heart, soul, mind, and strength. Such faith would involve, first of all, single-minded trust in God as the heavenly Father. The disciple cannot serve both God and things which are not God, Mammon. He can have only a single Master. He can only have treasure in one place, for where his treasure is, there will be his heart.

Single-mindedness, which Soren Kierkegaard, the nineteenth century Danish philosopher, identified with purity of heart, would affect one's life in all of its varied facets. It would eliminate anxiety about food and clothing and other necessities. The birds and the lilies offer object lessons concerning the Father's providence. If a disciple truly trusts him, he will stop worrying. If he "seeks first the kingdom of God and his righteousness," God will take care of the other needs (Matt. 6:33; Luke 12:31).

Single-mindedness will also rule out hypocrisy, play-acting,

in religious observance. A disciple of the kingdom is confident
of God's justification. Therefore, he does not have to put on
a show in giving alms, in prayer, or in fasting. The Father,
who scrutinizes the heart and not the external act, will repay
secretly one who gives secretly. Those who do alms for public adulation have already received their reward. Prayer,
likewise, takes place in the inner recesses of the heart. Piling
up words in prayer is a sign of smallness of trust. The true
prayer is that which leads one to forgive others as God has
forgiven him. Finally, fasting requires no external display but
only an internal resolve.

Single-mindedness will eliminate censoriousness. Judgment
belongs to God. One who trusts him whole heartedly will not
pick and find fault. His experience of divine love heightens
his awareness that whatever he is, it is of divine grace and not
of himself.

Like the Sermon on the Mount, Jesus' parables stressed
also that discipleship to Jesus is characterized by boundless
love and forgiveness. Like a person who has discovered a
hidden treasure or a pearl of inestimable value (Matt. 13:44-
46), the disciple is overwhelmed by this discovery. He will
do anything to obtain it. Experiencing this love and forgiveness impels him to love and to forgive. Indeed, the disciple knows that he has been justified if he loves and forgives:
if he has fed the hungry, given drink to the thirsty, welcomed the stranger, clothed the naked, visited the sick,
and cared for prisoners (Matt. 25:31;46). The disciple's love,
as the parable of the Samaritan shows, is boundless. So is his
forgiveness. Everything depends upon the genuineness of his
forgiveness of others (Matt 18:23-35).

The Final Consummation and the Church

Before concluding this discussion of the teaching of Jesus,
an additional word should be said concerning the Church in
the intention of Jesus. Whether Jesus intended the Church has
been much debated since Albert Schweitzer wrote *The Quest
of the Historical Jesus*. Schweitzer concluded that Jesus left

no place for the Church in his plan, for he expected the consummation to occur within his own lifetime (Matt. 10:23).
To this observation, which is in itself probably accurate,
others have added the argument that the two references to
Church (Greek *ekklesia* or Aramaic *qahal*) in sayings of Jesus
appear only in Matthew (16:18; 18:17) and, if authentic,
would have referred to the "assembly" of Israel, not the
Christian Church. Jesus, therefore, was concerned with the
kingdom of God, not with the Church.

Hardly anyone will now contend, against these points,
that Jesus envisioned the institutional Church as it now exists
or as it developed in the first few centuries. There is evidence,
however, to support the view that he did envision the Church
as the Remnant of Israel, or, as John W. Bowman stated, as "a
fellowship of those who share the Kingdom experience."

First of all, some direct sayings imply this. The group of
parables on fasting — the bridgegroom and his guests, the
new patch on an old garment, and the new wine in old wineskins — imply that Jesus expected some time to intervene
before the final consummation. Likewise, the whole catena of
passages in which Jesus called for allegiance to himself —
leaving family ties for the kingdom (Mark 10:29; Matt.
19:29); taking up a cross (Luke 14:27; Matt. 10:38; Mark
8:34); being hated and persecuted (Mark 13:13, parallels;
John 15:21; Luke 6:22; Matt. 5:10, 11, etc.); taking up his
yoke (Matt. 11:28, 29); and the parables of the strong man,
wicked husbandman, and rejected stone — clearly indicate
the gathering of followers who would continue his work at
least for a time. In addition, it has been pointed out that the
term "Son of Man," which Jesus probably used as a self-des-
ignation, had corporate implications. The Son of Man represented Israel.

Secondly, Jesus' challenges to faith indicate that he was
seeking to evoke a response not only to himself but also to
the Father. Such challenges would imply a continuation of
the people of God.

Thirdly, the calling of the Twelve, which in earlier discussion the writer ascribed to Jesus himself and not to the later Church, offers direct testimony of a continuation of the ministry of Jesus himself. This act was designed to teach the people that he would raise up a new congregation of Israel from this typical remnant.

Fourthly, the meals which he shared with his disciples suggest a continuing fellowship. The meaning of the Last Supper has been debated by scholars, and Jesus may not have commanded its repetition, as suggested by Paul (1 Cor. 11:24, 25). At very least, however, the meal symbolized the fellowship which would finally be enjoyed by those who would share the messianic banquet at the consummation. It was almost certainly not the only meal but one of several which Jesus shared with his disciples as he prepared them for his death.

Finally, Jesus' ethical teaching would have no meaning unless he envisioned a time in which it would have application. Unless one accepts Schweitzer's conclusion that it applied only to the future, it would suggest that Jesus envisioned a period of the Church before the consummation.

In the final analysis, there is probably no way in which one can or should remove the polarities in Jesus' thought. As a prophet, he agonized over the expectation of God's consummation of his purpose and thus foreshortened the time. At the same time he went on with God's mission for him. Urgently and impatiently he announced the presence of the kingdom of God in and through his own ministry. He challenged his hearers to enter it while time remained. As his own time grew short, he gathered a small circle, the Twelve, who would continue. He prepared them for discipleship in the kingdom. He gave them a new ethic for a new era, the era of the Messiah. That era dawned beyond the Cross.

6

The Death and Resurrection
of Jesus

The most definite fact about Jesus is his crucifixion. No Christian, surely, could have invented a tale of the ignominious death of the founder of Christianity. Of his resurrection perhaps, of his death no.

As clear as is the fact of the crucifixion, however, many other matters connected with it are subject to debate. One is the time and sequence of events which preceded and followed the crucifixion. Although the passion narrative of the Gospels was probably the earliest account of events in Jesus' life to be written down, the evangelists differed considerably on details, sometimes in rather significant ways. John and the Synoptics, for example, used different traditions concerning the date of the Last Supper, John evidently following a tradition from Asia Minor. Similarly, early sources contained two or more fundamentally different accounts of the Supper itself. Matthew evidently gave an expanded liturgical version of Mark's account (Matt. 26:26-29; Mark 14: 22-24). Paul (1 Cor. 15:23-25) recorded a different version. Luke, depending on whether one accepts the longer or shorter text of his account, either used a modified Pauline tradition (Luke 22:15-20) or possibly an independent tradition. John made no specific reference to the Last Supper as such, but he seems to have given an interpretation in the footwashing ceremony (John 13:1-20).

Another matter of debate is the reasons for the crucifixion. Like any historical event, the crucifixion is subject to varied interpretations, depending upon the slant of different interpreters. The Roman authorities, the Jewish religious leaders, the disciples, Jesus himself — all viewed it from diverse angles. Every subsequent Christian generation has read something of its own situation into the event. Small wonder, then, that modern interpreters give a variety of explanations concerning what happened.

Although there is little debate that Jesus was crucified, there is much debate concerning the claim that he was raised from the dead. Because this claim is so central to Christian belief, an essential, according to Paul (Rom. 10:9), conservative Christians have insisted upon acknowledgment of the resurrection *as historical fact*. While their concern for certainty is understandable, however, they are placing a burden upon historical evidence which it cannot bear. Through the centuries the Church has wisely made the resurrection *an article of belief*, not a statement of fact. To be sure, there is much evidence to support the belief. But to be proven historical fact the resurrection would require extraordinary evidence because it is a unique, never before or since attested phenomenon. What the historian can demonstrate, beyond reasonable doubt, is not the fact of Jesus' resurrection itself but the fact that it had a pronounced impact on the first believers. The evidence of this impact is direct and convincing.

This chapter is written, therefore, with an eye to critical discussion. The writer will draw conclusions carefully so as to avoid stretching the evidence farther than it should be stretched. Although the sequence of events is impossible to determine precisely, the one given in the traditional accounts is at least intelligible and logical.

The Passion
For the purposes of this book it will suffice to highlight four major stages in the passion narrative: the Roman interest in Jesus, the conspiracy of the Jews and Judas' betrayal,

the institution of the Last Supper, and the crucifixion. Around these the evangelists have gathered stories and sayings which filled out the accounts of Jesus' death.

The Roman Interest in Jesus

The crucifixion of Jesus raises many questions. Since the Romans crucified him, the proper place to begin asking these questions is: Why did the Romans put him to death? The answer to this question is fairly easy to ascertain. The evangelists agree that Pilate consented to have him executed as a potential revolutionary. In a land where revolutions sprouted with regularity a weak, half-competent governor like Pilate had reason to fear. Flaming Jewish nationalists threw off sparks which he could scarcely afford to ignore. His only question, therefore, was: "Are you the king of the Jews?" (Mark 15:2; Matt. 27:11; Luke 23:3).

Jesus' reply to Pilate, as recorded by the evangelists, was by no means a clear denial. Indeed, it appears somewhat evasive: "You have said so" (Mark 15:3) or "Do you say this of your own accord, or did others say it to you about me" (John 18:34)? An evasive reply naturally encourages one to ask whether Jesus may have been hiding his real intention. Was he a revolutionary?

Some scholars have recently put together a case for this view. They point to the fact that Jesus' disciples included a Zealot, Simon (Luke 6:15; Acts 1:13). Other disciples, for example, Peter, acted like Zealots. They also contend that the Romans would never have put Jesus to death had they not had good grounds for believing that he was a Zealot. If he were put to death for this reason, it is not difficult to suppose that his early followers rewrote the story so as to eliminate his actual Zealot activities and to relocate the blame. They could have invented Pilate's reluctance to put him to death and sought to shift the blame to the Jews. Then they could have imposed the Servant image upon Jesus prior to the crucifixion so that it would appear that he had a completely different kind of messiahship in mind all along.

Although a few have found this theory convincing, most

scholars reject it for several reasons. First of all, it presupposes a massive rewriting of evidence by the early Christians, who, on the whole, can hardly be considered so sophisticated. If they wanted to rewrite the story, would it not have been easier to deny the crucifixion altogether? Second, it conflicts with the rather consistently represented view that Jesus himself rejected the Messiah ben David image and projected the image of a Messiah-Servant. Although the early Church could have read the latter image into his mind in retrospect, it is more feasible to suppose that such a unique concept originated with Jesus himself, not some committee of interpreters. As indicated in an earlier chapter, there is no reason to believe that Jesus could not have foreseen his death, even if not crucifixion, as a result of growing antipathy between himself and the Jewish religious leaders. That kind of antipathy, third, stands out not merely in the overt sayings and deeds but shows through the parables, which no doubt reflect the most authentic thoughts of Jesus himself. It is not likely that the early Church invented the subtle responses to Jewish religious leaders which those parables reflect. The life situations into which the evangelists placed them show quite different concerns on the part of the Church. Fourth, the presence of a Zealot among Jesus' disciples proves nothing about his own intentions. His intimate followers obviously had varied interests and concerns which he informed. The fact is, all of his followers seem to have misunderstood him, wanting to impose a quite different type of messiahship, but he resisted their interpretations.

In the final analysis, it seems wise to accept the view of the evangelists that the Romans were interested in Jesus chiefly because of a possible threat to the peace. Jesus did have a following. At times this following may have seemed large enough to foment a revolution. Some followers viewed him as a Messiah like David. The fact that Jesus would not openly and straightforwardly deny messianic claims jeopardized his situation. Without encouragement from his enemies, however, it is unlikely that this situation would have worsened to the point of causing his condemnation.

The Jewish Conspiracy and Judas' Betrayal

Since Hitler's effort to exterminate the Jews, there have been extensive efforts to eliminate insofar as possible the anti-semitism of Christian writings, especially the Gospels. Numerous studies have proven that the evangelists "slanted" the story in such a way as to make the Jewish people, particularly their leaders, culpable in the death of Jesus. Were they?

It can hardly be doubted that they were less guilty of chicanery than the evangelists sometimes implied. The Gospel of John particularly implied a general conspiracy on the part of the "Jews," virtually isolating Jesus from his own ethnic heritage. The term "Jews," however, had a broader application in John, alluding to virtually any opposition. Such a general opposition among Jewish people can hardly have existed, for Jesus was popular with the masses. As the Synoptists saw the matter, it was not at all popular antipathy but that of the sects and parties who saw in him a threat to their vested interests which resulted in a conspiracy to have him put to death. Opposition to him and his ministry came from several different sources.

One source may have been Herod Antipas, Tetrarch of Galilee and Perea, before whom Jesus appeared before Pilate passed final judgment (Luke 23:6-16), and Herod's strong supporters. Mark, at any rate, reported that the Pharisees counseled with the "Herodians" regarding Jesus' death (Mark 3:6; Matt. 12:14; cf. Mark 12:13). Herodian concern may have stemmed from Jesus' association with John the Baptist (Mark 6:14 ff.) Jesus himself had warned his disciples about "the leaven of the Pharisees and the leaven of Herod" (Mark 8:15). Like the Pharisees, Herod had a concern for the Law.

A second source was the scribes and Pharisees, zealots regarding the punctilious observance of the Law, ritual as well as moral. The reason for their hostility to Jesus stands out clearly in the Gospels: Jesus threatened the entire set of rules which they had put together as the means by which the re-vealed will of God could be obeyed. Jesus never questioned the seriousness of their intent, but he did question whether their handling of the Law helped anyone to arrive at the mark. Their system of rules produced not sons of God but "sons of the Gehenna" (Matt. 23:15).

In contrast to the scribes and Pharisees Jesus emphasized the deeper intentions of God for men. To arrive at these intentions, he not only interpreted the Old Testament writings differently, but he claimed also to stand above the Old Testament. He could correct Moses! It was precisely this attitude toward the Law which the scribes and Pharisees found insufferable. They rightly perceived that such an attitude would undermine not only their system of rules but the Law itself. Implicitly or explicitly, he was claiming to speak for God, an assertion of authority which they thought blasphemous. They had much to lose if Jesus' approach prevailed.

It is not difficult to believe, therefore, that the scribes and Pharisees may have participated in a plot to put Jesus out of the way. Allowing for exaggeration by the evangelists of the sinister manner in which they went about this, one still can believe that some of them grew increasingly agitated over his critique of their casuistry. They could well have used their influence to have him executed.

A source of opposition which was more directly responsible for Jesus' death was that of the Sadducees, the priestly aristocracy. This opposition was connected less with the Law than with the Temple. As regards both doctrine and customs, the Sadducees were perhaps more tolerant than the Pharisees. They were not tolerant, however, about disruptions of the Temple and its institutions. Whatever else it may have signified, the cleansing of the Temple by Jesus represented a flagrant trespass on the authority of the priestly aristocracy. The violence with which Jesus proceeded possibly led to the distorted conclusion that he intended to destroy the Temple. At any rate the accusation which the chief priests lodged against him was that he said, "I will destroy this temple that is made with hands, and in three days I will build another, not made with hands" (Mark 14:58; Matt. 26:61; cf. John 2:19). Against the accusation Jesus offered no rebuttal.

The Jewish Sanhedrin which tried Jesus indicted him for blasphemy. The grounds for this were twofold: his statement regarding the destruction of the Temple and his claim of messiahship. Some scholars contend that the charge of blasphemy in Jesus' day was restricted to saying the divine name, YHWH, of whose pronunciation we cannot be certain. Insofar as formal evidence of customs in the first century is concerned, this view may be accurate. It is not difficult to believe, however, that a hostile court could have expanded the charge. His citation of the Son of Man saying from Daniel 7:13 came dangerously close to a direct claim of divinity, and, as the writer contended earlier, Jesus' assertions of authority in both deed and word did so even more. Jesus was not claiming messiahship merely in terms of the descendant of David motif but much more in terms of the heavenly Son of Man who comes on the clouds. All the religious leaders needed to confirm their suspicions of exaggerated claims of authority was this citation.

A fourth source of opposition was the Jewish nationalists, Zealots, who at one point probably believed that Jesus was the long-awaited Davidic Messiah. Jesus did and said many things to encourage at least some, like Simon, called the Zealot, to follow him. He evidently faced a constant temptation to yield to their pressures. When some of them began to discern clearly that he was not going to be their kind of Messiah, they began to pull away and possibly to see in him a threat to their own aims, the restoration of the Davidic kingdom.

A disappointment of this kind probably figured significantly in Judas' betrayal of Jesus. To be sure, other motives may have accompanied and reinforced this one. One which Matthew's account suggested was monetary. According to

Matthew, it was Judas who approached the chief priests with a demand for money (Matt. 26:15). This interpretation is reinforced by John's view that it was Judas, not others among the apostles, who objected to the use of costly ointment in the anointing of Jesus at Bethany. Indeed, John directly accused Judas of being a thief and embezzler of funds (John 12:1-8). Against this interpretation of Judas, however, stands the more positive view of Judas presented in Mark and Luke. The chief priests, not Judas, proposed remuneration for the betrayal (Mark 14:11; Luke 22:5). This more positive assessment is reinforced by recollecting that Judas would hardly have followed Jesus as he did had he not had more noble motives, for discipleship to Jesus involved complete renunciation.

It seems better to suppose that Judas betrayed his master out of disappointment when he discovered that Jesus was not going to be the kind of Messiah he expected, a Messiah ben David. Judas may have been the first of the disciples with whom Jesus' passion predictions really registered. The others were slow to comprehend. Indeed, they resisted what Jesus was forecasting about himself. Jesus' anointing at Bethany could well have been the occasion when the light dawned for Judas. If so, he no longer wanted to be a party to a suicidal mission.

The Last Supper

The last meal which Jesus shared with the disciples seems to have been the setting for his final disclosure of this mission to them. It was doubtless only one of many such fellowship meals, but it held a significance which the others could not have held. Like other incidents in the life of Jesus, however, it is difficult to reconstruct what took place. The accounts pose several problems.

One problem is the date. John placed the meal one day earlier than the Synoptics, on Nisan (March-April) 14 rather than Nisan 15, Passover eve. The difference in these traditions became the occasion of a controversy during the second century. Churches in Asia Minor followed John's chronology, most other churches followed the Synoptists'. John may have altered the date for theological reasons or because he used a different calendar, for example, like one discovered at Qumran.

A more serious problem is whether the Last Supper was a Passover meal or not. Already by Paul's day the early churches regarded it as a Passover meal, and all four Gospels agreed. A number of objections to this view have been raised, however, on the basis of the accounts: the fact that Jesus did not use unleavened bread as required for Passover (Mark 14:22; 1 Cor. 11:23); the omission of any mention of the paschal lamb and bitter herbs; the use of a common cup, whereas individual cups were used at Passover; the arrest of Jesus on the night of Nisan 15, which Jewish law forbade; and several other events which could not have taken place on Nisan 15, according to Jewish law. These objections may be weakened somewhat by recognizing that Jewish law was not as rigid in the first century as has sometimes been supposed. Moreover, there are a number of positive evidences that the Last Supper was a Passover meal: its observance in the evening and extending into the night; the reclining position of Jesus and the disciples, whereas the Jews ordinarily sat at meals; a dish preceding the meal, which occured only at Passover; the drinking of red wine as required by Passover regulations; the concluding of the meal by a hymn as at Passover; the departure of Jesus to the Mount of Olives rather than Bethany as allowed by Passover regulations; and Jesus' narrative at the meal, which resembled the Passover *Haggadah*.

To resolve obviously ambiguous and perhaps contradictory evidences, scholars have proposed several other theories. One is that the Last Supper was a sabbath-*kiddush*, at which the head of a household said a prayer of sanctification (*kiddush*) over a cup of wine and drank it along with other members of the household. Another is that it was a simple fellowship meal, called a *Haburah*, which friends often shared with one another. A third connects it with the meals at Qumran, which used red wine and pointed to the banquet of the last days. While all of these theories have some merit, however, each leaves as many questions unanswered as it answers. It is probably sounder in the long run to accept the early tradition that the Last Supper was a Passover meal and to assume that some conflicting evidences could be resolved if first century Jewish customs were better known.

A third problem has to do with the form of Jesus' words. This problem is complicated by question regarding Luke's text. Some ancient manuscripts of Luke delete Luke 22:19b-20, which corresponds to 1 Corinthians 11:25. If the shorter version of Luke was original, then Luke knew a tradition of the Lord's Supper like that found in a writing not included in the present New Testament called *The Teaching of the Twelve Apostles* (*Didache*). The tradition placed the cup before the bread. In this way Luke's version would agree neither with that of Mark and Matthew nor with that of Paul.

The Lucan problem aside, there is still the question of a difference between Mark's and Paul's accounts. Matthew, of course, reproduced Mark's version with little alteration. Many scholars argue that the brevity of Mark's version and its Aramaisms make it more original than Paul's. Others, on the contrary point out that Mark contains Aramaisms throughout, so that this would not necessarily sustain originality.

A final, perhaps most thorny, problem is one of interpretation. Even supposing that he could solve all of the other riddles and find the very words of Jesus himself, the historian can give no dogmatic answer to an issue which has divided Christians for centuries. The key words found in Mark 14:22, 24, "Take; this is my body" and "This is my blood of the covenant, which is poured out for many," almost certainly alluded to Christ's approaching death as a sacrifice of atonement, like the Passover lamb which had already been slain. The Aramaic which Jesus spoke would have had no copulative. Bread and wine, therefore, it would be accurate to say, "represented" the sacrifice of Christ as the true paschal lamb. His death would seal a new "covenant" between God and his people. It would have validity not just for his disciples but "for many." "Many" can be interpreted as meaning "all," Aramaic having no word for "all."

The words in 1 Corinthians 11:24 and Luke 22:19, "Do this in remembrance of me," may not have been Jesus' words. They could, however, have represented his wish.

The remaining words, Mark 14:25, "Truly I tell you that I will no longer drink of the fruit of the vine until the day I drink it new in the kingdom of God," were essentially an oath. Jesus vowed to consummate what he had begun. Like the passion sayings, the Last Supper looked beyond death to victory given by God.

The Crucifixion

Some elements of the passion narrative sound like theological reflections by the first generations of Christians, but many others have a ring of authenticity. Would later generations, for instance, have made up the words of Jesus in the Garden of Gethsemani, "Abba, Father, all things are possible to thee; remove this cup from me; yet not what I will, but what thou wilt" (Mark 14:36)? The ministry of the Messiah-Servant was reaching its climax. Would they have invented the account of Peter's denial (Mark 14:66-72)?

Pilate sentenced Jesus to death for insurrection in place of Barabbas. The custom of releasing one prisoner annually is unknown except from the Gospels, but the Romans were known to exercise such magnanimity at times. Barabbas was a prisoner charged with the same crime as Jesus (Luke 23:19).

The abuse which Jesus received in the course of his trial and crucifixion would have been customary for persons convicted of serious offenses. Scourging (Mark 15:15) was a horrible form of beating meant to weaken the prisoner and hasten death, and it would help to explain why Jesus faltered carrying the cross and then expired within six hours. The mocking of the Roman soldiers was the kind of thing one would expect under the circumstances. The powerful Romans liked to make sport of the troublesome Jews.

The place of the crucifixion is often disputed. From A.D. 336 on, when Constantine's mother Helena had a church erected there, the traditional site has been the Church of the Holy Sepulchre. The actual location depends largely upon the location of the walls mentioned by Josephus. The crucifixion had to take place outside the walls of Jerusalem. Today the holy sepulchre is a small cell, six feet by six feet, which has been altered by marble face on the rock and lamps hung from the ceiling. On one side is a solid stone shelf five feet by two feet by three feet. The cell is entered by a low door. Near the entrance is a set of stone steps leading to the hill of Golgotha. The Church has been erected over the rock surface of the mound.

In 1867 a British army officer, G. G. Gordon, discovered a site outside the Damascus Gate in the north wall of Jerusalem which some have since espoused as the site of the crucifixion. It is a cliff weathermarked or quarried in such a way as to resemble a human skull. Nearby is a "Garden Tomb" which some contend was the burial site. A groove has been cut in front of the door, possibly to slide a stone across the opening. Inside there is one completed shelf. Many archaelogists agree on a first century date of construction.

The crucifixion occured at 9:00 a.m. This method of execution was cruel, reserved for runaway slaves and the worst kinds of non-Roman criminals. The victim could either be tied or nailed to the cross while it was laying flat on the ground. Then cross and victim would be hoisted up and dropped into a deep hole. The pain grew as time passed. Wine mixed with myrrh served as a drug which could ease the pain (Mark 15:23). But Jesus' cry of dereliction would have been the cry of deep human suffering. Death usually resulted from strangulation as the body sagged further and further.

The Resurrection

Some would write the *finis* to the story at that point. To do so, however, would not explain the origins of Christianity. However noble Jesus' teaching, however meritorious his life, neither would have sufficed to overcome the ignominy of the crucifixion had his followers not believed he had risen from the grave.

There are two types of evidence for the resurrection of Jesus — the empty tomb and the appearances. As the writer indicated earlier, neither of these can be viewed as "proof" in the sense that testimony to other historical happenings can be considered "proof" because of the uniqueness of the resurrection. Both, however, substantiate the profound conviction of the first believers that Jesus did not remain in the grave but entered into a new order of existence.

The Empty Tomb

Many scholars believe the empty tomb evidence began to be used later than the evidence of experience. That judgment is sustained by the fact that Paul made no mention of the empty tomb in 1 Corinthians 15 or elsewhere. Mark alone, in what many believe to be a fragmentary ending (Mark 16:1-8), cited the empty tomb exclusively. Matthew, Luke, and John included both evidences.

How much credence can the historian give to the empty tomb stories? In itself the absence of Jesus' body from the tomb would seem to have been confirmed by Matthew's report that the chief priests bribed the soldiers to say that the disciples came at night and stole his body while they were sleeping (Matt. 28:13). Furthermore, Mark's account is so matter-of-fact and unembellished that it is difficult to discredit.

These facts notwithstanding, attempts were made early on to explain away their implications. Cerinthus, an early Judaizing Gnostic of Asia Minor, theorized that the Christ who descended on Jesus at baptism left him at the cross. Thus, the body laid in the tomb was Jesus', not the Christ's. Others, including one or two modern authors, have speculated that the Essenes stole Jesus' body and spirited it away after restoring it to life.

In the end, the historian has to confess uncertainty. But the empty tomb evidence is strong enough to require serious attention.

The Appearances

The reports of appearances fall into another category than the reports of an empty tomb. For one thing, comparison of various accounts show embellishment in response to the skepticism of critics both within and outside the Christian movement. Luke and John, for example, both had the risen Christ supply manifest proof that he was real, not just a phantom, evidently against the docetists, those who denied the reality of the physical. In Luke 24:39: "See my hands and feet, that it is I myself; handle me, and see; for a spirit has not flesh and bones as you see that I have." In John 20:27, Jesus, responding to the doubts of Thomas, challenged, "Put your finger here, and see my hands, and put out your hand, and place it in my side; do not be faithless, but believing." Along similar lines, Luke had Jesus eat fish as evidence of his physical reality (Luke 24:42).

Although embellishments like these deserve to be treated with caution, clashing as they do with other evidences, the very existence of the Christian movement depended upon an authentic and profound experience which lay behind even the embellishments. The earliest and no doubt most reliable accounts of this experience can be found in Paul's letters, in which he cited not merely his own experience but a tradition which concurred with and reinforced it. The tradition which Paul cited in 1 Corinthians 15:3ff. listed what for any other historical event would be overwhelming confirmation. Witnesses included Peter (Cephas); the Twelve; "more than five hundred brethren at one time, most of whom are still alive, though some have fallen asleep;" James; "all the apostles;" and finally Paul himself. The fact that the resurrection was more than a historical event, a "supra-historical" event as it were, however, takes it beyond the historian's purview. It thus moves into the realm of faith.

It is possible, however, to ask: "What did these first believers experience?" Again, the accounts differ enough to rule out a definitive answer. Some, obviously, wanted to view the resurrection in the crassest and most literal terms. Some at Corinth, for instance, expected an exact replica of the human form (1 Cor. 15:35-36), an expectation which undoubtedly derived from Jewish apocalyptic. That expectation recurred in the encounter with docetists (those who denied that Jesus was really human) when the second century creed included belief in "resurrection of the *flesh*." On the opposite extreme of the spectrum, others spiritualized. Resurrection did not wait until the end. It had occurred already, perhaps in baptism or through spiritual enlightenment of some kind (2 Tim. 2:18). This view suited better the Hellenistic expectation of immortality.

Paul sustained neither of these views, and it is perhaps safest to reconstruct the experience of the first believers from him, since the matter was of crucial significance for him and his apostolate. Paul was convinced that the Christ who appeared to him belonged to another order of existence than the Christ the disciples had known in the flesh. The risen Christ had not a physical but a spiritual body. Flesh and blood, Paul contended, cannot inherit the kingdom of God. The perishable physical nature has to give way to the imperishable spiritual nature.

If any connection can be made between Paul's experience of Christ's appearance to him and that to other disciples, which for Paul was crucial and essential, then the appearances were more in the nature of theophanies, like the Old Testament theophanies of Yahweh. This would explain why, on the Emmaus road, for example, the disciples failed to recognize Jesus until he did something familiar to them. And so he has often appeared to men at other times and in other places. This does not mean, however, that modern experiences are just like those of the first believers. Paul, at any rate, believed that his own experience of the risen Lord was out of the ordinary. It was a delayed birth, an appearance to "one untimely born" (1 Cor. 15:8). He did not expect a repeat for someone besides himself.

The details of what happened in these appearances lie beyond the historian's competence to evaluate. What did Jesus instruct? What did he command? One has no way of confirming or denying these private experiences. The first followers may have mistaken some of the instructions and commands. But there can be no doubt that it was their powerful conviction that he had risen which sent them out from Jerusalem, to Judaea and Samaria, and to the ends of the then known world.

PART THREE

"Into All the World"

7

Primitive Christianity

Some scholars would begin the story of Christianity with the resurrection rather than the life of Jesus. In some respects this would be a reasonable approach, for Christianity did indeed spring from the experience of the resurrection. Despite all of its connections with Judaism and even with Jesus' earthly ministry, it could never have become a self-conscious movement had the first followers not believed that Jesus was raised and appeared among them again. The resurrection belief alone explains a remarkable emergence from the gloom of the crucifixion.

The first Christians gathered in separate coteries, according to the Book of Acts, because they shared a common experience. What set them apart from their fellow Jews was not a system of theological beliefs but an experience, an experience which convinced them that Jesus was the long-awaited fulfillment of Israel's messianic hopes. They met in the Temple and they met privately in homes to proclaim that Jesus of Nazareth, the crucified one, had been raised from the dead by God to be both Messiah and Lord. In short, with his resurrection the messianic age had dawned. It was time to repent, believe this good news concerning Jesus' death and resurrection, and participate in the life of Israel under the new covenant.

So long as this message fell only to Jewish ears, it caused no difficulty. It was not long, however, before it reached a wider audience, that of proselytes and godfearers and then even that of the "godless" Gentiles. It reached their ears freed of the narrowing strictures of the Jewish ritual and moral law, and thus threatened the twin pillars of Judaism. For Christianity it was fateful that the man charged most directly with stamping out this threat was converted to the faith he persecuted and thus became the chief architect of the mission not merely to Jews but to Gentiles as well. Within a generation Christianity freed itself from the restrictive bonds of Judaism and became a universal faith, not bound by circumcision or other marks of Judaism.

The Sources

The period under discussion lasted from about A. D. 30, the death of Jesus, to A. D. 70, the fall of Jerusalem to the Romans. Knowledge of it comes chiefly from Paul's letters and the Book of Acts. Unfortunately neither of these sources gives an exact chronology. Of the two, Paul's letters, whose number is debated, undoubtedly supply the most direct and reliable information obtainable about the period. Some scholars, however, view some letters with suspicion and believe that Paul himself wrote no more than two-thirds of them. Chronology too is debated. The earlier letters were the two written to Thessalonica, or possibly Galatia. Next came the Corinthian letters, followed by Romans, Philippians, Colossians, Philemon, and possibly Ephesians. The so-called Pastoral letters — First and Second Timothy and Titus — are widely regarded as in whole or in part post-Pauline. So also is Ephesians.

Acts contains some sources which are very early. It supplies a chronology first of early Christianity before Paul and then of Paul. This chronology, however, does not coincide fully with the one which can be reconstructed from Paul's letters. It is necessary, therefore, to make many educated guesses about the progress of Christianity during the first forty years of its existence.

For the sake of clarity it seems wise to treat the story in

terms of three foci. The first was Jerusalem, site of Jesus' death and resurrection and springboard for the spread of Christianity to other centers of Judaism. Until A. D. 70 Jerusalem retained a central place in the life of the Christian church, but the destruction of the Temple in that year meant an inevitable shift to other centers. Standing in the wings, ready to assume that place, was Antioch, which had already distinguished itself as the launching platform for the mission to the Gentiles. Until Jerusalem fell, Antioch wore the mantle of a subordinate of Jerusalem. Thereafter, however, it was free. Meantime, Greek-speaking Jews in Jerusalem grew discontented with second-class Christian citizenship. Led by Stephen, they pressed for a break with the ritual and legal strictures of Judaism, especially circumcision of males. Stephen's plea in behalf of an unhindered mission to the Gentiles incited a reaction on the part of those who saw the covenant in narrower terms. Fortunately, the one-time leader of this opposition, Saul of Tarsus, became the new focus of the mission to the Gentiles. By his death in the sixties Christianity had been planted in virtually every important center of the ancient world. It was not vigorous and strong, but burgeoning persecution here and there failed to wipe it out.

Jerusalem

The first center of the Christian movement, not unnaturally, was Jerusalem. It was in Jerusalem that Jesus had brought his mission to a climax. It was in Jerusalem that he died. And it was in Jerusalem that he first appeared to some of his followers, although one ancient tradition contained his promise to precede the disciples to Galilee (Mark 14:28; 16:7; Matt. 26:32; 28:7). At any rate numerous appearances occurred in Jerusalem.

The Message

The beliefs of the primitive community cannot easily be reconstructed. Some of their chief emphases, however, have been preserved in what C. H. Dodd has called "the apostolic preaching." At the heart of these beliefs was the conviction that God had raised the crucified Jesus from the dead and thus made him both Lord and Messiah (Acts 2:36). The confession of Jesus as Lord equated him with Yahweh in the Old Testament, where the tetragrammaton was rendered by the Greek *Kyrios*, Lord. It was predicated upon the unshakeable conviction that God had raised him from the dead, upon the experience of the Spirit in the Christian community (Acts 2:36-38), upon the use of the Old Testament in Christian exegesis, upon Jesus' use of the term Lord in his parables and in the question concerning David's son (Mark 12:35-37), and upon the effects of the invocation of Christ in worship, excorcism, and baptism.

The primitive preaching was adapted to different audiences, but C. H. Dodd included the following elements: The age of fulfillment has dawned (Acts 2:16; 3:18, 24). This took place through the ministry, death and resurrection of Jesus (Acts 2:30-31; 3:22; 2:23ff.). By virtue of the resurrection, Jesus has been exalted to the right hand of God as messianic head of the new Israel (Acts 2:33-36; 5:38). The Holy Spirit in the Church is the sign of Christ's present power and glory (Acts 2:33, 17-21). The messianic age will shortly reach its consummation in the return of Christ (Acts 3:21; 10:42). Repent, receive forgiveness and the Holy Spirit, and salvation ("the life of the Age to Come") by entering the elect community (Acts 2:38-39).

Organization

The Jerusalem community had an organization unlike that of any other churches founded at later times. Presiding over it was the Twelve, Matthias being elected to take Judas's place (Acts 1:23), a council of elders, and a group of three apostles accorded special recognition — Peter, James, and John. James, the brother of Jesus, assumed a special place of leadership as time went on which some have compared to episcopal authority. It was he, for instance, who sent out the famous Jerusalem decree (Acts 15:13). In addition, the whole assembly passed judgment regarding some matters.

The primitive Jerusalem community obviously held an extraordinary esteem in the eyes of other churches due to its connection with the ministry and death of Jesus. The churches of Judaea, Samaria, and Syria, for example, felt constrained to check with Jerusalem concerning the validity of work among non-Jews. Barnabas went as a special emissary to Antioch to evaluate the addition of Gentiles to the church there (Acts 11:19-22). Later, Paul and Barnabas, though commissioned by the church at Antioch, went regularly to Jerusalem to report on their missionary activities in Asia Minor. And it was in Jerusalem that the so-called "Jerusalem Conference," which probably occurred in A. D. 49, determined that Gentiles could become Christians without first becoming Jews by circumcision. Exactly what stipulations were made are unclear, for early manuscripts give two quite different texts. Neither of the texts required circumcision, but one may have required adherence to ritual customs while the other required only adherence to moral requirements of the Law (Acts 15:19-20).

The discovery of the Dead Sea Scrolls in 1947 led to some intriguing speculation about the influence of the Essenes upon this organization. The Essene community at Qumran was governed by a council of twelve laymen plus or including three priests presided over by a *mebaqqer* or superintendent. The whole community, the "many," took part in disciplinary matters. Could these correspond to the Twelve Apostles, the three "pillars," and James? The correspondence may be more than accidental, for, according to the Qumran *Manual of Discipline*, the Council of Twelve Laymen and Three Priests were "to set the standard for the practice of truth, righteousness and justice, and for the exercise of charity and humility in human relations; and to show how, by control of impulse and contrition of spirit, faithfulness may be maintained on earth; how, by active performance of justice and passive submission to the trials of chastisement, iniquity may be cleared, and how one can walk with all men with the quality of truth and in conduct appropriate to every occasion."

The analogies are intriguing. It must be pointed out, however, that Qumran was a monastic community arranged in rather strict hierarchical fashion, whereas early Christianity was not. Further, James assumed his place more or less by virtue of his kinship with Jesus. No other person succeeded him as head of the community. The Twelve, too, were unique, the foundation of Israel under a new covenant. The "three" purely *ad hoc*, not continuous. If Qumran did have an influence upon the Jerusalem organization, it did not have a continuing impact in later times, for Christian organization elsewhere took quite different forms.

Worship

It is clear that at the outset the earliest disciples continued as a sect of Judaism. They frequented the Temple and participated in its worship. They offered sacrifices and observed the calendar prescribed by Jewish law. They gave offerings for the poor. Save for some separate gatherings on the Porch of Solomon, north of the Temple courtyard (Acts 3:11), no one would have noticed anything singular about their habits. For many of them the destruction of the Temple in A. D. 70 evoked tears.

Outside of Jerusalem, likewise, believers frequented the synagogues and participated in the traditional rites — reading the scriptures, sermons, prayers, and the rest. Indeed, the spread of Christianity depended upon the tilling of the field by Jews outside Palestine. Wherever Christian missionaries went with their tidings concerning the Messiah, they knew they could find a receptive audience. It is less clear than some suppose, as a matter of fact, that Christianity broke with the synagogue in A. D. 70. The continued expansion of Christianity necessitated an ongoing encounter with communities of Jews scattered throughout the Roman world.

At the same time Christian belief that the messianic era had dawned in the death and resurrection of Jesus, symbolized by the outpouring of the Spirit at Pentecost, made mandatory some special observances which would eventually bring a cleavage between the Church and Judaism.

One of these observances was a fellowship meal, called by Paul the "Lord's Supper." Several questions arise in connection with this meal. *One is how often it occurred.* In Acts 2:46 Luke stated that the Jerusalem Christians broke bread in their homes "day by day." If the Lord's Supper was meant, it would appear that it occurred daily. Willy Rordorf has contended, however, that the meal took place weekly on "the Lord's day." The term "the Lord's Day" derived from eating the "Lord's Supper" at "the Lord's table." *Another question is what the observance entailed.* Judging by 1 Corinthians 11, the whole observance was an actual meal concluded by the symbolic rite which Christians today call the eucharist or Lord's Supper. This meal had a charitable intent. The "have's" brought food and drink for the "have not's." Later on, this was called *agápe* from the Greek word meaning "love" or "charity." Abuses such as those mentioned by Paul (1 Cor. 11:20-22), 2 Peter 2:13, and Jude 12 led to the separation of the symbolic observance from the charitable meal. The *agápe* meal, however, was continued as a private observance until at least the sixth century.

The symbolic portion of the meal probably imitated the Last Supper, as Paul indicated in 1 Corinthians 11:24, 25. However often it was observed, it held an unusual amount of significance for the first believers, a significance which even the Last Supper could not have held for the apostles. Like the latter, it looked back upon Jesus' death "on behalf of many." It was much more than a remembrance in the modern sense of the English word, however. It made the believer a part of the event, a sharer in the death of Jesus on his behalf, just as the one offering a sacrifice would have shared in his own offering. Equally importantly, it involved the participants in a present fellowship with the risen Lord. This was the Lord's Table, according to Paul, meaning that the risen Christ presided over it just as he had presided over the Last Supper. Nothing the Christian could do, therefore, could speak more profoundly of his *koinonia* with his brethren. In this meal the participants became the Body of Christ. That is why the self-ishness of some Corinthians directly contradicted the nature of the meal itself. It was not the "Lord's Supper" which they participated in at all (1 Cor. 11:20). Finally, the symbolic meal pointed forward toward the consummation of God's redemptive work in Christ. It prefigured the heavenly banquet which all believers would share with him in the final consummation.

It is clear, then, how the Christian meal differed even from the Last Supper. The latter, like the meal at Qumran, *pointed forward* to something; the Christian eucharist *pointed backwards*. It was a joyous celebration because the age which John the Baptist and Jesus had been proclaiming had dawned with death and resurrection of Jesus. This did not mean a complete and final victory over evil, but it did mean that a decisive event had occurred which would assure that victory. This was, as Oscar Cullman has observed, the D-Day which preceded V-Day.

Fellowship

Another thing which set Christians apart from their peers in Judaism was the intimacy of their fellowship, in Greek *koinonia*. This intimate fellowship produced two side-effects.

One of these was community of goods. The community of goods was not based upon a theoretical ideal of a perfect society. To the contrary, it was a sharing which resulted from a *koinonia*, a fellowship, which touched the deepest levels of human existence. Those who owned possessions sold them and distributed the proceeds to all "as any had need" (Acts 2:45). Luke presented a beautiful picture when he remarked that "the company of those who believed were of one heart and soul, and no one said that any of the things which he possessed was his own, but they had everything in common" (Acts 4:32). He was honest to confess, however, that the community had both Barnabases and Ananiases and Sapphiras.

Another effect was discipline. Acts offers several instances of severe cases of discipline in the Jerusalem community. In the case of Ananias and Sapphira, however, their deaths represented a divine judgment rather than a community action. In the case of Simon the Magician, the apostles acted quickly and severely to exclude an offender. The chief case of discipline, however, had to do with requirements for membership in the community of the new covenant. Would it be circumcision and obedience to Jewish rules, or would it be Christ alone?

Healings and Signs

The Jerusalem community of believers stood out in the final analysis for its demonstration that the messianic age had dawned through healings and other signs. The age of the Messiah was, of course, to be an age when the Spirit would fall upon all in an unusual way. Those things which Jesus did, therefore, his followers did.

Altogether these observances set Jesus' followers apart from their fellow Jews. Their numbers grew, first among the Jews and proselytes, then among godfearers, and finally among non-Jews. So long as they attracted Jews only, there was no serious problem. However, their fellowship, their charities, their deeds of mercy could not long stay within the confines of Judaism. The crumbs increasingly dropped from the table among the "puppies." As they were lapped up by eager Gentiles, the question of mission loomed larger and larger. Could anyone become a Christian unless he first became a Jew? Some said yes. Some said no. A rift was inevitable.

Breaking the Bonds of Judaism

Christianity did not easily break free from Judaism. As a matter of fact, the rupture was not intentional, and it came as much from the Jewish side as from the Christian. Many, perhaps most, Jewish Christians, including Paul, intended to remain within their ancestral faith. They understood, and correctly so, that Jesus had confined his and his disciples'

mission to Israel and only reluctantly allowed it to trickle beyond. He also criticized the Pharisees' proselytizing. How,
then did the break occur?

Jesus himself prepared for this by removing the idea of
vengeance from the Jewish mission and by promising the
Gentiles a share in the eschatological salvation. That salvation, he may have foreseen, would occur beyond the cross,
through his voluntary submission to God. Thus after the
resurrection, however understood, he bound his disciples to
complete what he had begun through his death and resurrection.

For some, reared in Jewish ancestral traditions, the only
route to the promises God had made to Israel would be
through Judaism, adopting both ritual and moral customs.
The main core of the Jerusalem leadership — James, Peter,
John and the others — seems to have taken this stance at first.
James, who earned the respect of the Pharisees, tiptoed about
with great caution. Peter, though brash and precipitous in
some ways, vacillated back and forth, now favoring and now
avoiding contacts with Gentiles. At Antioch Paul openly
rebuked him for slipping away from a meal with Gentiles
when some Jews from Jerusalem caught him in their presence
(Gal. 2:11-12). Others, understandably, were squeamish
about contravening ancestral rules. Even Barnabas, noted
for his level-headedness, backtracked under pressure from
conservatives.

The breakout from Judaism came, therefore, from Hellenistic rather than Palestinian Jewish sources. This was to be
expected, for Hellenistic Judaism had already gone a long
way toward accomodating to Hellenistic culture. Philo of
Alexandria, for example, had "found" the finest Greek philosophy in the Pentateuch. Moreover, non-Palestinian Jews
were content to employ Greek language and idiom. Many
imitated Greek customs. They frequented the baths. They
read Greek literature. They enjoyed Greek theater. They
wore Greek dress.

There was preparation, then, for the break from Palestinian Jewish customs. In primitive Christianity two persons were particularly responsible for the actual break. One was Stephen, the other Paul.

Stephen, according to Acts, was a Hellenistic Jew "full of grace and power" who "did great wonders and signs among the people" (Acts 6:8). His message was interpreted by other Jews as an attack upon "Moses and God" or "this holy place (the Temple) and the law" (Acts 6:11, 14). It was the same charge which the Jewish sanhedrin had made against Jesus. The speech which Luke attributed to Stephen reveals that he was contending that God never confined himself either to a particular place (the Temple) or to a particular people (the Jews). God "does not dwell in houses made with hands" (Acts 7:48), and the Jews did not keep the Law which he delivered to them (7:52-53). The result was Stephen's stoning.

Paul was also a Hellenistic Jew, a native of Tarsus in Cilicia, Asia Minor. At one point he led the effort of Pharisaic Judaism to wipe out the Christian movement. His hostility to the movement is self-evident; he was fearful, as were many others, that Christianity would destroy "the traditions of my fathers" (Gal. 1:15). Accordingly, he persecuted the church violently and tried to destroy it.

But Paul changed. The persecutor became the leader of the mission he tried to halt. Why?

Paul himself does not relate a dramatic conversion like the one recorded by Luke in Acts 9 and elsewhere, which some have associated with an epileptic seizure. He leaves no doubt, however, that he experienced a sudden, profound, irrevocable conversion. God "revealed" his Son to him (Gal. 1:16). Paul experienced the risen Christ in the way other apostles had experienced him, even if later than they (1 Cor. 15:8). He, too, was an apostle, even as they, because he had seen the risen Lord (1 Cor. 9:1). He was "caught up to the third heaven" and given an "abundance of revelations" (2 Cor. 12:2, 7).

In this meeting with the risen Lord Paul became at the same

time the apostle to the Gentiles. No human being commissioned him as an apostle, not even one of the other apostles, but Christ himself (Gal. 1:1). He was an "apostle of Christ Jesus," the last and the least of the apostles because a persecutor, but still an apostle. Even the Jerusalem apostles recognized that God had made him apostle to the Gentiles, Peter the apostle to the Jews (Gal. 2:7-8).

Stephen's bold step followed by Paul by no means cleared the debris from the path of the mission to the Gentiles. Throughout Paul's missionary journeys he encountered sustained opposition from a group he labeled "Judaizers." This group insisted upon circumcision of males and observance of the Jewish ritual as well as moral law. The more Paul and his company attracted Gentile converts, the stronger the opposition of the Judaizers grew. They threw up as many roadblocks as possible to stop the Gentile mission. In the end they had much to do with Paul's arrest and eventually with his death.

Paul's opponents do not deserve the serious censure which they have sometimes received. They expressed a legitimate and commendable concern, namely, conservation of the integrity of their ancestral faith, the same concern Paul once held. They feared the kind of accommodation in which, under Paul's leadership, Christianity proceeded to engage. Would abandonment of traditional marks of Judaism, for example, circumcision of males, go so far as to mean abandonment of everything the Law implied? Would Christianity end up being not at all unlike the hodge podge of religions which competed with one another in the Roman world? How could Christianity retain identity unless it held to the Law as Judaism held to it? All of these were important questions, and answers did not come easily. For some Paul himself did not give a satisfactory answer.

Pauline Christianity
Paul was unquestionably, save for Jesus himself, the most

important single figure in the beginnings of early Christianity. Some would even label him the founder of Christianity. Such a view is clearly erroneous, but he was almost that important. He was the bridge over which Christianity moved from the Palestinian Jewish setting to the Hellenistic world. Without him the story of Christianity would surely have been quite different than it was.

Paul the Missionary

Before looking at the message, instruction and baptism, organization, worship, and discipline of churches founded by Paul, it will be useful to look at the missionary himself. Born in Tarsus, he was educated in Jerusalem under Gamaliel II (Acts 22:3), ordained a rabbi, and became a member of the sect of Pharisees (Phil. 3:5). By his own admission he was a zealot about the observance of the Law (Gal. 1:14). When Christianity began to pose a threat to the Temple and the Law, he received a commission from the chief priest to seek out and arrest those who belonged to the movement in Damascus and to return them to Jerusalem, a commission he discharged with fearsome fervor (Acts 9:2, etc.). His conversion, however, intervened to change all of this. He became a zealot for the Christian mission instead.

It evidently took Paul considerable time to sort out the meaning of his conversion experience, which most scholars date around A. D. 32 to 36. He went first to Arabia, probably meaning the desert area near Damascus, and then returned to Damascus. Three years later, he went to Jerusalem to confer with Peter and James the brother of the Lord. Then he went to the province of Syria and Cilicia, presumably to do mission work around Tarsus. After a considerable period of time, according to Acts 11:25, Barnabas brought Paul from Tarsus to Antioch to assist in the work there. At this time, presumably, Paul made his second visit to Jerusalem with Barnabas and Titus to take a relief offering on account of the famine in Judaea (Acts 11:29-30). According to Paul, this was fourteen years either after his conversion (or after the first visit). The missionary journeys began a short time later.

Paul had a clear strategy for his missionary work. He intended to plant a church in each of the Roman provinces, usually in a significant city, stay long enough to see the seed sprout, and let the good news spread out from the young plant like flower runners. His long-range goal was the planting of churches from Jerusalem to the farthest reaches of the West, which for him meant Spain (Rom. 15:24), wherever churches did not exist (Rom. 15:19-20).

The missionary journeys are usually divided into three, but such a division is artificial, distinguished only by brief returns to Antioch and Jerusalem. The *first* journey covered territory familiar to Barnabas and Paul. Barnabas led the missionary party through Cyprus. Paul led it through Pamphylia, Pisidia, and Galatia in Asia Minor. He concluded with a visit to Antioch and Jerusalem to report on the benefits of the mission. At this juncture the so-called Jerusalem Conference gave ambiguous consent to the mission. The *second* journey retraced part of the steps of the first. In it Paul obviously intended to head for Ephesus, a center of commerce and culture, but was compelled, for unexplained reasons, to head northwards. Fortuitiously he crossed into Europe, going through Macedonia and Achaia and settling for a year and a half in Corinth. Still intent upon work in Ephesus, he made a fleeting trip to Jerusalem and returned to Ephesus to spend about three years. As a result, perhaps, Ephesus became the strongest center of Christianity in the second century. The third missionary journey involved a retracing of Paul's steps through the cities of Macedonia and Achaia to collect the offering he was making for the impoverished Christians of Jerusalem. His hope was that this offering might provide a final proof of the validity of the Gentile mission, but his hopes seem to have proven vain.

Paul's final visit to Jerusalem proved fatal for him personally. On the charge that he brought a Greek, Trophimus of

Ephesus, into the forbidden part of the Temple, he was arrested (Acts 21:29). An appeal to Roman citizenship alone saved him. The Romans spirited him away to Caesarea, where he spent about two years in prison before finally making the arduous trip to Rome (Acts 27-28).

Paul's last days are uncertain. Despite imprisonment by being chained to a Roman soldier, he continued his missionary witness (Phil. 1:12-14), evidently with some success. Early tradition attests that he was released after a trial, made a journey to Spain and elsewhere, was rearrested, again tried, and then beheaded during the Neronian persecution (A. D. 64-68).

The Message

At one time it was fashionable for New Testament scholars to accentuate Paul's originality, and of that there can be no question. More careful study of the sources, however, has shown that, despite his emphasis upon a unique call and commission, Paul relied heavily upon earlier tradition, the substratum of the Christian message, as it were. He himself frequently mentioned the "traditions" which he handed on to churches which he founded. He could commend the Corinthians, for example, because they remembered him in every respect and maintained the traditions "even as I have delivered them to you" (1 Cor. 11:2). Or he could exult that the Romans, whom he did not know personally, had become "obedient from the heart to the standard of teaching" to which they were committed (Rom. 6:17). The fact is, Paul tested his own experience over against that of those who were apostles before him; what he insisted was that his teaching coincided with theirs (Gal. 1:18; 2:9).

What did Paul's inheritance include? One part of it was either certain Old Testament testimonia or "text plots" which were used to prove Christian doctrine. Collections of proof texts, testimonia, were in existence by the mid-third century, for Cyprian of Carthage compiled one, but scholars still debate whether any existed in the New Testament era. There were at least, as C. H. Dodd maintained, certain seedbeds for gathering proofs from the Old Testament.

Another part of this inheritance was hymns or confessions of faith. Paul's letters contain a number of these, the crucial one perhaps being 1 Corinthians 15:3ff. Paul explicitly designated this as a tradition:

"For I delivered to you as of first importance what I also received, that Christ died for our sins in accordance with the scriptures, that he was buried, that he was raised on the third day in accordance with the scriptures, and that he appeared to Cephas, then to the twelve. Then he appeared to more than five hundred brethren at one time, most of whom are still alive, though some have fallen asleep. Then he appeared to James, then to all the apostles. Last of all, as to one untimely born, he appeared also to me."

Here was the *sine qua non*. Besides it, however, Paul cited numerous other snatches of tradition which filled in tiny bits of information about the underlying foundations of his theology: Romans 1:3-5; 4:24b-25; 10:9; the Faith-Hope-Love triad; Philippians 2:6-11; Ephesians 5:14; and numerous other passages.

A third part of this inheritance was catalogues of virtues and vices. Subsequently these catalogues became the basis for the "Two Ways" instruction of early Christianity — the way of life and the way of death.

A fourth part of this inheritance was the household codes which supplied instructions concerning relationships between slaves and masters, children and parents, young and old, husbands and wives, etc. Paul's letters contain at least three sections usually designated household codes: Romans 13:1-7, Colossians 3:18-4:1, and Ephesians 5:22-6:9.

Paul's letters also included allusions to words of Jesus, early Christian proverbs, doxologies, benedictions, and numerous miscellaneous allusions.

The presence of all of these materials in Paul's letters confirms that he was not the innovator in theology some have supposed. He was creative, to be sure, but his creativity stemmed from the way he fed these materials through his own fertile mind and redirected the Christian message toward a new audience, one more accustomed to Hellenistic modes of thought.

At the heart of Paul's thought, scholars have long recognized, was the phrase "in Christ." To be "in Christ" had for him both personal and ecclesiastical significance. The new convert was baptized into Christ, that is, into the death of Christ (Rom. 6:3; Gal. 3:27). There was a certain mystical aspect involved in the experience. It meant "putting on" Christ as one's new personality, laying aside the old habits and characteristics and donning new habits and characteristics. But it meant also being united with others in the Body of Christ, a new type of humanity (1 Cor. 12:13). Being in Christ signified having characteristics which one had not had "in Adam." In place of alienation, it meant reconciliation. In place of hatred, it meant love. In place of pride, it meant humility. In short, it meant all the virtues or fruits of the Spirit which should characterize the life of the Age-to-Come.

Paul did not mention the kingdom of God often as Jesus did. It is evident, however, that he understood this concept under other rubrics. God's rule was becoming reality within the Body of Christ. Here the fruit of the Spirit prevailed over the life of the flesh. "Love, joy, peace, patience, kindness, goodness, faithfulness, gentleness, self-control" (Gal. 5:22-23) were supplanting "immorality, impurity, licentiousness, idolatry, sorcery, enmity, strife, jealousy, anger, selfishness, dissension, party spirit, envy, drunkenness, carousing, and the like," such things as prohibited one from inheriting the kingdom of God (Gal. 5:19-21).

Like Jesus, Paul, too, centered the Christian ethic on the concept of *agápe*-love. The law is summed up in one statement, "You shall love your neighbor as yourself" (Rom. 13:9). Indeed, "Christ is the end of the law, that every one has faith may be justified" (Rom. 10:4).

Paul's great contribution was to free Christianity from the strictures of Judaism — circumcision, food laws, fastings, and even rigid moralism. More clearly than any of his contemporaries, he made personal commitment to Christ the single essential for Christian faith. How is a person justified? he asked. Not by works of law, circumcision or any other, but solely by God's gracious act in Christ. By his death upon the cross Christ has freed us from sin and death and from the curse imposed by the law. "For by grace you have been saved through faith; and this is not your own doing, it is the gift of God — not because of works, lest any man should boast" (Eph. 2:8-9).

In the Jewish world such a conclusion may have created no problem. In the Gentile world it did. To many Gentiles the promise of forgiveness which Paul made was an invitation to license. If God justifies one no matter how great his sin, should he not sin all the more in order to enjoy more grace? Some queried. But Paul answered with a resounding no. Whoever has received much forgiveness should be freed from the desire to sin. Whatever he may have been, he has been washed in baptism, sanctified, and justified "in the name of the Lord Jesus Christ and in the Spirit of our God" (1 Cor. 6:11).

Protestants and Catholics have long debated the meaning of Paul's word "to justify." Protestants have stressed its juridical nature, as a declaration of acquittal in the last Judgment. Catholics, however, have interpreted it as an act in which the believer is made right. Careful study of Paul's usage shows that both of these interpretations are correct. God transforms the believer; he "rightwises" him. Thence the convert should do what is fitting of God's righteousness. In the present life, however, no one, even the believer, does what is right always. His salvation, therefore, still awaits God's merciful forgiveness and acquittal.

Like other Christians of his day, Paul envisioned himself as living between the times of Chirst's comings. The eschatological age had dawned with the death and resurrection of Christ. The Spirit had been poured into the hearts of believers. Together they formed the Body of Christ, the fellowship of the redeemed. They had the urgent task of proclaiming the good news of what God had done in Christ. The time was short. Soon the Lord himself would descend from heaven and consummate that which he had begun.

It is debated as to whether Paul modified his expectations about the final consummation. First and Second Thessalonians clearly indicate that he preached the immediate return of Christ, so fervently in fact that some at Thessalonica ceased all activity in order to wait for the Parousia (2 Thess. 3:10). The delay of the return of Christ, however, evidently forced him to moderate his views. Although he still earnestly hoped that the Return would occur before he died (2 Cor. 5:4), he realized that he could not set the schedule. He would have to wait for the time set by God. Meantime, those who died "in Christ" before the return could expect to share the resurrection experience with those who still lived. The dead would be raised first, then those who were alive would be caught up to meet with Christ in the air (1 Thess. 4:16-17; 1 Cor. 15:51-52).

In the Hellenistic world this message of forgiveness of sins and the promise or participation in new life struck a welcome note among the despairing and oppressed masses. Paul could use familiar analogies to talk about liberation from the power of Sin and Death, tyrants now vanquished by Christ. Christ freed the slaves of sin like benefactors manumitted slaves from the slave masters. Risen from the dead, he proclaimed victory over Death and Hell. God had given victory!

Instruction and Baptism

Wherever Paul went he founded communities of believers who would continue and expand the work which he had begun. He trained a core of those who could hand on to others what they had learned from him. As he envisioned these communities, they would function in the manner of an organism directed and controlled by the Holy Spirit. The Spirit would apportion the work of the Body as needed. In short, the church would be essentially spirit-filled and spirit-directed.

Converts in Paul's churches went through an instructional period of undeterminable length. There was a special group of persons charged with instruction (1 Cor. 12:28, 29). Whether this occured before or after baptism has been debated. In the Jewish context, where extensive preliminary instruction could be presupposed, it seems to have followed baptism. In the Gentile context, however, it soon preceded baptism, although perhaps not in Paul's day.

Whenever it occurred, this instruction had a rather formal character, for Paul himself spoke of a "standard of teaching" (Rom 6:17) and "traditions which you were taught by us" (2 Thess. 2:15). It undoubtedly included such things as the writer named earlier: confessions, hymns, words of Jesus, catalogues of virtues and vices, household codes, and numerous other elements. The new believer was carefully equipped for his life in the world.

Baptism, as the key rite of initiation into the Body of Christ, had an import which many persons today would fail to catch. For Paul it dramatically symbolized the death and resurrection of Christ. It was an acted parable, as it were, of the believer's participation with Christ in both death and victory over death. As death could not hold sway over Christ, neither can it hold sway over those who follow him in the death of baptism. Baptism demarcated the line between the old age and the new, between the old life and the new. In baptism the resurrection to the life of the new age already began.

Structure

Since the late-nineteenth century, debate has raged fiercely concerning the structure of churches founded by Paul. Because of Paul's stress on Spirit control, the noted German jurist Rudolf Sohm argued that Paul intended nothing but charismatic leadership, the type evidenced in 1 Corinthians 12. In this letter Paul gave no indication that there were formal "offices." He spoke, rather, of functions — apostles, prophets, teachers, and several undefined functions (1 Cor.

12:28). Sohm went on to contend that formal offices represented a departure from the true nature of the Church, which was essentially spiritual. Such a departure occurred with the Letter of Clement of Rome to the Corinthians, composed in A. D. 96, when presbyters and deacons became formally and legally constituted offices.

Many persons have replied to Sohm's theory. Its chief weakness is whether the Church can ever be a "purely spiritual entity" such as he envisioned, as Adolf Harnack noted. Even for Paul, it surely misreads the evidence. In 1 Corinthians 12:28, first of all, Paul enumerated three of the functions or offices, obviously intending to assign special places to them. Despite a delay of Christ's return, moreover, it is difficult to believe that any congregation functioned without some order of a more formal kind. Indeed, one of the "functions" listed in 1 Corinthians 12:28 was that of "administration." Third, this view neglects evidence of other letters which bear Paul's name.

First and Second Timothy and Titus may have been written by a disciple of Paul, so the writer will not cite the clear evidences for formal offices which they present. Philippians, however, falls into a different category, and Paul's allusion to "bishops and deacons" in the preface can hardly be ignored. This evidence implies that, whatever may have been the case in Corinth, some Pauline churches had a two-fold pattern of church office. The Greek term *episcopoi*, translated bishops, almost certainly described the function of presbyters.

If 1 and 2 Timothy and Titus were genuine Pauline writings, they confirm the same two-fold pattern in other Pauline churches (Ephesus and Crete) or, according to some interpreters, the three-fold pattern of presbyters, deacons, and bishop. This writer, however, favors the view that the term "bishop" in 1 Timothy 3:1 was a generic term for presbyter and that the author knew only two offices.

A question which these data raise is: Was there development and what prompted it? Quite possibly, as Sohm contended, Paul may have started with the intention of founding "purely spiritual" congregations. This would accord with his conviction that the messianic age was the age of the Spirit and that the Spirit alone should rule. The Spirit means freedom! It must be recalled, however, that Paul won his first converts in and through the Jewish synagogues. The synagogues already had a structure which corresponded in many ways with the bipartite structure of the church of Philippi. If a large portion of the constituency of a synagogue were converted, Paul could not easily have shifted the structure. Since it was his principle to let minor matters ride in order to obtain larger goals, he could well have accepted whatever structure seemed to fit the circumstances. Thus, at one and the same time, some Pauline churches may have operated charismatically while others took over the structure of the synagogue. In the latter cases the office of deacons would have been added to complement the already existing office of presbyters.

Worship

It has already been pointed out that Christians made no immediate break with Judaism, not even in A. D. 70. According to Acts, however, Jewish reaction to Christian preaching in the synagogues frequently precipitated rejection and expulsion. For obvious reasons the latter created the occasion for the development of Christian special forms of worship. Some scholars, such as Gerhard Delling, have used this fact to argue that Christian worship reacted against rather than imitated Jewish synagogue worship and thus was characterized particularly by novelty.

It is true that some special Christian observances did develop. One of these, discussed earlier, was the Lord's Supper, though even it was not without precedent. Another, which seems to have occurred in churches founded by Paul, especially Corinth, which should not necessarily be taken as normative for all of Paul's churches, was a spirit-filled, prophetic worship in house churches. It must be remembered, of course, that the first believers did not have and did not try to build special buildings for worship. These came in time, to be sure, but they were not feasible in the first several generations when Christianity was an illicit religion in Roman eyes. Further, Christians believed that the time was short. Christ would soon return to earth. Presently they needed to concentrate upon spreading the good news as quickly as possible.

These essentially prophetic services included several elements. One was *prayer*, evidently of a more or less spontaneous variety. From the first, however, Christian prayers included some set elements which have partially survived in the New Testament and other early writings — the address of God as *Abba*, Father; the *Amen* at various points in the services; doxologies; benedictions, hallelujahs; and other elements taken over from Judaism. Another was *singing*. Colossians 3:16 mentions "psalms, hymns, and spiritual songs." Psalms perhaps included both Old Testament and Christian psalms. Hymns and spiritual songs were probably fresh creations of the Church, some spontaneous and some more carefully planned, like 1 Timothy 3:16. Another was *scripture reading*, which Paul called "a lesson" (1 Cor. 14:26). These perhaps included both Old Testament readings and letters, like those written by Paul or other apostles. Another was *prophecy*. Prophecy was intelligible speech under inspiration of the Spirit, perhaps closer to spirited preaching than to mysterious utterances. Finally, there were *tongues and interpretation of tongues*. Here Paul urged caution and placed intelligent speech far above unintelligible because it edified the whole assembly more.

Fellowship and Discipline

Like the Jerusalem churches, Paul's churches, too, experienced something of the intimate fellowship which characterized the body of Christ. This fellowship resulted in commendable acts of charity toward not only fellow Christians but even non-believers. It also allowed encouragement, admonition for faults, rebuke, and even exclusion from the fellowship.

At this early stage discipline chiefly entailed "shunning" offenders, that is, avoiding them at Christian gatherings. Paul forbade even table fellowship, presumably at the Lord's Supper, a prelude to excommunication, with persons guilty of serious offenses. But he held more moderate views of those who committed less serious breaches of fellowship. For those who repented restoration after forgiveness occurred immediately (2 Cor. 2:5ff.).

The offenses which evoked discipline included chiefly moral wrongs, as in the case of the man at Corinth who had an incestuous relationship with his stepmother (1 Cor. 5), or breaches of fellowship. Theological aberrations entered the picture later, unless one regards the letters to Timothy and Titus as Paul's.

Around A. D. 70

The picture of Christianity which emerges around A. D. 70 is a variegated one. Beginning in Jerusalem, it had spread by various means throughout the known world, both East and West, North and South, in the path of Hellenistic Judaism. If Luke's listing in Acts 2:5-11 implies anything about the spread, it shows that Christianity stretched from Mesopotamia to Rome and from the Black Sea to Libya. It is hardly likely, however, that the scattered communities of believers represented anywhere more than a tiny fraction of the populace. The strongest contingent was probably in Jerusalem, Antioch, Ephesus, and Rome.

Beliefs, organization, and worship observances varied. True, there existed a basic substratum focused upon testimony about the life, death, and resurrection of Jesus. New converts learned some basic traditions. But the new communities had no single discernible pattern of organization. Jerusalem, with James as leader, approximated an episcopal pattern. Corinth tended more toward congregational polity. Other churches adopted the two-fold structure of presbyters and deacons. However, no modern denomination may suppose that its structure corresponds closely to any of those exhibited by early Christianity. Rites of initiation also varied. In the Jewish setting new converts may have been instructed following baptism. As the church moved into the Gentile world, however, instruction may have preceded baptism. Worship varied, too. Jerusalem Christians continued to worship in the Temple. Outside Jerusalem, they frequented the synagogues. At the same time they developed their own special services — the Lord's Supper and the prophetic service.

However much moderners may idealize diversity, there is a natural tendency toward uniformity. In a few years the manifold structures and customs of widely scattered Christian communities moved in the direction of uniform structures and customs. Diversity gave way to catholicity.

8

Catholic Christianity

By A. D. 70 Christianity did not cut a prominent figure on the religious scene of the Roman Empire. A century or so later, however, it began to emerge as a noticeable phenomenon and as a subject of discussion in Roman polite society. Indeed, it was significant enough to provoke a few pagans to draft an attack upon Christianity and an apology for paganism.

This change of status calls attention to a number of concomitant changes during these hundred years. The obvious change was numerical. Substantial numbers of Christians lived in Alexandria and parts of Egypt, in Antioch and Syria, in Edessa, in Ephesus and parts of Asia Minor, in parts of Greece, in Rome and parts of Italy, and even in north Africa, especially Carthage.

Change in numbers was accompanied by a change in constituency. Whereas at first the converts were mainly Jews and Jewish proselytes, later ones were coming more and more from among Gentiles. Furthermore, whereas Christianity's charities and its fellowship without regard to race or social standing meant that the majority of the early converts came from the lowest levels of society, now it began to attract a few educated and cultured peoples. One charge frequently leveled at Christians in these early years was the fact that they attracted so few people of "consequence" and "reputation." Paul himself could testify that, among converts in Corinth, there were reformed adulterers, homosexuals, thieves, drunkards, revilers, robbers, and the like, such people as could expect no inheritance in the kingdom of God (1 Cor. 6:9-10). Many converts were slaves and poor freedmen. Little by little, however, Christianity began to attract some from a higher social station.

Change in constituency necessitated a change in the character of Christianity's apologetic and proselytizing efforts. At the outset Christianity competed chiefly with the oriental mystery cults in attracting converts. As people of higher station manifested interest in it, however, it began to adjust its appeal upwards in the direction of the philosophies. It was presented not just as one among the philosophies but as the philosophy, the true philosophy.

As one would expect, changes were also taking place institutionally and theologically. The simple forms of the early period no longer sufficed to allow Christianity to discharge what was becoming an increasingly worldwide, "catholic," mission. The influx of large numbers of Gentile converts forced developments: in initiation procedures, in worship, in disciplinary measures, in structures, and in thought.

Since the Protestant Reformation, Protestants have tended to look askance at these developments. Authentic Christianity, in the view of many, was apostolic Christianity in its unvarnished simplicity. Later developments, therefore, represented distortions and perversions of the original intention of Jesus and his first followers. Thus an effort has been made to recover the thought and customs of the apostolic era.

One can appreciate a concern which is expressed in this attitude, that is, a concern to see that accretions of later centuries do not obscure and distort what lies at the essence, even if the essence cannot be isolated in the raw. At the same time, however, he recognizes fully the necessity of institutional development and regards most developments as authentic. The fact that some distortions, for example, an excessive legalism in pastoral care, occurred should not occasion a loss of confidence in all development, either in doctrine or practice. A study of the history of early Christianity as well as a look at the Church today confirms the absolute necessity of development.

The story of early Christianity's growth and development in this period, about A. D. 70 to 200, is a complex one, hindered by large chronological gaps in information. The part which is told here will be sketchy but perhaps enough details can be included to provide the reader with a fair picture. For the sake of clarity the story will be divided into three parts — the church and the world, diversity and division, and institutional development.

The Church and the World

The world which challenged early Christianity was described earlier. What must now be told is how Christianity evangelized and related to the Roman Empire, which increasingly became its home.

The Spread of Christianity

It would be futile to try to compile statistics, but Christianity spread throughout the Roman Empire and beyond with remarkable rapidity. It did so by several agencies. One was soldiers, sailors, merchants, slaves, and others who traveled throughout the Empire both by land and sea. Archaeological excavations have turned up evidences of Christian witness in the remotest parts of the ancient world by A. D. 200.

Another was the planting of churches. Begun by apostles like Paul and his colleagues, church-planting was unquestionably the chief means for the spread of Christianity. What Paul began continued through the work of Timothys, Tituses, Sylvanuses, Priscillas and Aquilas, and thousands of others. It was evidently the Pauline method of planting churches in centers of commerce, population, culture, etc. in a province which produced later the diocesan structure of early Christianity.

A third was apologetic or evangelistic schools. These may have begun as catechetical schools or on private initiative. In the mid-second century Justin founded such a school in Rome, evidently on his own initiative, attracting persons to Christianity in much the same fashion Stoic, Epicurean, Platonist, or Peripatetic philosophers attracted pupils. Such schools may have followed the lead of Gnostics like Valentinus, Heracleon, and others, who also used schools to spread their teachings. The most noted of the schools was one founded in Alexandria by a certain Pantaenus and made famous by Clement and Origen. All three of these were philosophical evangelists.

Another means for the spread of Christianity was its charities, opened to all without strings attached. Rome did not lack charities, but few of these reached the persons who most needed them, the truly indigent. Around A. D. 250 Cornelius of Rome testified that the Roman church had 1500 needy persons, that is, besides clergy, on its dole. Such generosity cannot have failed to have attracted thousands.

Persecution

Prior to a kind of detente between the Church and society which began to emerge with Gallienus about A. D. 260 and then became more clearly established with Constantine, the relations between Christianity and Roman society were at best strained. The success of Christianity in winning adherents from among the Roman populace frequently incited harassment, mob reaction, and occasionally official persecution. No official, organized, universal persecution occurred, however, until the mid-third century, when the Emperor Decius finally realized that Christianity had become a quasi-state within the state and thus a threat to his own control.

The first persecution erupted under Nero, A. D. 64, and remained more or less localized in Rome. By admission of all witnesses in this case Christians were scapegoats for the emperor's half-mad attempt at urban renewal by burning down half the city of Rome. Hysteria seized the city, so that many innocent victims perished, being covered with pitch and serving as human torches for the arena at night, being gored by wild beasts, being eaten by lions, and being fried in huge frying pans.

The second persecution, under Domitian, A. D. 91-96, spread to the provinces and was most fervid in Asia Minor, where Christianity obviously had its greatest numbers. Here there were cries of "atheism," for refusal to acknowledge the gods of Rome. Among the martyrs were Flavius Clemens, cousin of the Emperor, his wife Domitilla, and Acilius Glabrio, an exconsul. Obviously Christianity was beginning to ascend the social ladder.

The third persecution occurred under the Emperor Trajan, A. D. 98-117. It was evident that by this time anonymous accusations frequently led to the deaths of non-Christians as well as Christians. Trajan tried to avert this policy by making careful stipulations concerning execution of a more cautious policy. His famous *Rescript* provided (1) that Christians should not be sought out and anonymous accusations should be ignored, (2) that only those regularly accused and who admitted to being Christians should be punished, and (3) that those who denied that they had been Christians or insisted that they had ceased to be Christians and proved this by offering the prescribed sacrifices should be pardoned. This Rescript remained in force until the time of Septimius Severus (193-211). The one notable martyr under Trajan was Ignatius, the Bishop of Antioch.

In two subsequent periods of persecution the Emperors Hadrian (117-138) and Antoninus Pius (138-161) reiterated the first two provisions of Trajan's Rescript. Under Antoninus the most notable martyr was Polycarp, Bishop of Smyrna, who was burned in A. D. 156.

A sixth period of persecution occurred under the Stoic Emperor Marcus Aurelius. This persecution might seem anomalous in a number of ways, for Stoics, indeed Marcus himself, had much admiration for Christians, particularly for their discipline. Marcus, however, probably realized the burgeoning strength of Christianity, which was being talked about in circles he frequented, and thus repeated the third provision of Trajan's rescript. Many martyrdoms occurred in Africa and Gaul. Among the more prominent martyrs were Carpus, Papylus, and Agathonica; Justin of Rome and his companions; the martyrs of Scilli, and the martyrs of Lyons.

More deliberate, organized, and intensive persecution began under Septimius Severus (193-211). A new series of edicts regulated persecution. Christians were no longer accused by private prosecutors but sought out by the state. Septimius punished not only the newly converted but also their converters. Among the well-known martyrs were Saturus and his pupils Perpetua and Felicitas and some companions.

The severity of persecution between A. D. 70 and 200 has often been exaggerated, largely because Christianity was numerically weak. Proportionately few died as martyrs, far fewer than died in the era of the Inquisition or the Protestant Reformation. Actually the Romans tended to be tolerant, and the Empire knew a hodge podge of cults. Why, then, was Christianity singled out almost exclusively for persecution? There were doubtless several reasons.

At an early time one factor was the ill-will of the Jews, who resented Christian encroachment upon the synagogue. Another was the superstition of the heathen, who ascribed natural calamities to the fact that Christians failed to worship the gods. Another was the fact that Christianity tended to divide families. Some family members became Christians; others did not. Another was the social and economic disruption caused by Christianity. Christianity sowed the seeds of decay for the institution of slavery. It tended also to encourage voluntary poverty, although that was not noticeable until the fourth century. Another was popular misunderstanding of Christian rites and ceremonies. Such phrases as "the kiss of peace," allusions to "eating the body" and "drinking the blood" of Christ, and nocturnal meetings led to popular

charges of cannibalism and incest. Another was Christian exclusivism. Some Christians refused to occupy certain offices
— teaching, political office, armed service — and to attend
public games and activities. The ruling classes viewed these
attitudes as political threats and the masses as hard-headed
individualism. Christians also formed *collegia*, exclusive
societies, for burial, which invited suspicion by rulers. Finally, there was Christian loyalty to a law and throne besides
that of Caesar. This was a most serious threat to Rome. All
things had to be subordinated to the state in order to main-
tain its security. To a Roman, obedience to the state cultus
was a matter of patriotism; to a Christian, it was idolatry.
Christians could not claim anyone but Christ as Lord.

The Apology for Christianity

Although the severest persecutions came in the next
period, the period now under discussion was the crucial one
for the development of an apology for Christianity. Christian
apologetic literature was so extensive that no effort will be
made to catalogue it. It varied greatly in quality and effec-
tiveness. Generally speaking, early apologies concentrated
on answering charges, later ones on developing a positive
argument for Christianity. The apologists clearly grew more
sophisticated in their ability to do both.

It is possible to single out apologies both to Judaism and to
Hellenism. In the early period, for obvious reasons, an
apology to Jews was chiefly at stake. But this apology inter-
twined inextricably with that to Gentiles, for one major
objection of Romans to Christianity was that they, while
worshipping the Jewish God, did not observe all Jewish customs. To understand the reply to Gentiles, therefore, it will
be helpful to look at the apology to Jews.

The Jews objected to Christianity on several grounds: (1)
use of the Greek version of the Old Testament called the Sep-
tuagint, which was not a very literal rendering of the Hebrew
and contained writings not found in Hebrew; (2) the claim
that Jesus was Messiah; (3) the claim that Jesus was God; (4)

the Christian contempt of Jewish ritual observances such as fasting, the sabbath, etc.; (5) the doctrine of a crucified Messiah; and (6) the doctrine of resurrection. In response to the first objection Christians produced new versions of the scriptures, very literal ones rendered by a converted Jew named Aquila and another named Symachus. The others were met by arguments from scriptures. To these, Christian apologists added a clincher argument to prove that Christians were now the true people of God. This entailed citing the facts of history, namely the dispersal of the Jewish people, the destruction of the Temple, the cessation of sacrifices, the disappearance of the Jewish monarchy, and the reception of the gospel by the Gentiles.

Gentiles also made several charges against Christianity: (1) moral debasement, (2) social aloofness, (3) theological absurdity, (4) atheism, (5) treason, and (6) responsibility for the calamities and decline of the state. The apologists met the first charge by citing facts and explaining what actually occurred in Christian gatherings. Some turned the charge by remarking that pagans would never have thought so ill of Christians were they not guilty of such things themselves. The apologists had to accept the charge of social aloofness, but they turned it into an argument in their favor. After rejecting at first the sarcastic suggestion that they thought themselves a "third race," they used it to contend that the tag fit, for they were different in their customs, above all, morally. Apologists employed divergent approaches to charges that some doctrines, for example, the resurrection, were absurd. One group, for example, Tatian, argued that the uniqueness of Christian doctrine substantiated its authenticity. Others, however, sought to find analogies in contemporary thought.

The charges of atheism, treason, and responsibilities for calamities befalling the Empire were closely interrelated. The charge of atheism was based not on the fact that Christians believed in no God but on the fact that they did not believe in the gods. Sometimes the apologists rejected it outrightly, but more often they moved in two directions. One was to argue from both Greek philosophy and Hebrew prophecy for monotheism. The other was to point out the absurdity of polytheism, the immorality of Greek mythology, and the failure of Greek philosophies to correct this mythology. The political charge associated with the charge of atheism was difficult to answer directly. Christians had to admit that they could not worship the emperor and offer the prescribed sacrifices. They went on to say, however, that they were model citizens, paid their taxes, and, better than worshipping the emperor, prayed to the God who would assist the emperor. In the end, they contended, these things would aid him more than perfunctory observance of the state cultus. Finally, the apologists' answer to charges that Christians were responsible for natural calamities and the decay of Rome lay in the development of a philosophy of history. This began in the second century, but it reached its classic stage with Augustine's *City of God.*

Impact and Attitudes to the Graeco-Roman World

The impact of Christianity in this era, given a relatively limited constituency, cannot have been marked. By A. D. 200, in areas like Alexandria, Antioch, Ephesus, Rome, and Carthage, where possibly a tenth of the population was Christian, some social effects might have been observed. Generally speaking, however, Christianity was making its mark more noticeably in this era on individuals and on small groups of those who belonged to its ranks. Indeed, its converts expressed varied attitudes toward the "world," whether that meant the philosophies, religions, or social customs of the day.

Many took a very negative view. Clement of Alexandria, for instance, knew some who contended for "faith alone" and wanted to pronouce a not too-polite curse upon the world. Tatian, a Syrian who studied under Justin in Rome, wanted as little as possible to do with philosophy, which he regarded as "the art of making money." Tertullian demanded to know what "Athens" (Greek culture) had to do with "Jerusalem" (Christian culture) and opined that Christians had to live with pagans but they didn't have to sin with them. In actuality, he imbibed pretty deeply of the best culture Rome had to offer.

Others took a much more positive view of Hellenistic culture and led Christianity toward a significant accommodation. Valentinus, Heracleon, Basilides, and many others usually labeled "Gnostics" took the largest and most fearless steps in this direction. However, Justin of Rome and Clement of Alexandria led the way in a rather positive and perhaps salutary accommodation with the finer elements of Hellenistic philosophy. Justin himself was, of course, a person of rather limited culture. He argued, but weakly so, that Christianity was the "true philosophy." The divine Logos, who taught both the Greek greats and the Old Testament prophets, had become incarnate in Jesus of Nazareth. Now humankind at last had the perfect teacher. Clement, a person of rather obscure background, perhaps an Athenian, took the same thought a step farther than Justin. Flourishing around 190 to 202 in the Alexandrian School, he spoke of two pedagogues leading to Christ, both schooled by the divine Logos. One was Greek culture (especially Plato's), the other was Hebrew culture (especially the prophets'). If one took all the fragmentary bits of truth which he could find in those two streams and put them into one, he would have the truth itself. That truth, in fact, became incarnate in Jesus of Nazareth. He is *the* Teacher. Clement went somewhat further in the footsteps of Gnostic precursors when he distinguished two or three levels of enlightenment which the believer may attain. One is the level of simple faith, where one grasps the bare rudiments. The other is the level of *gnosis*, where one goes intuitively into higher truths, mysteries which the ordinary believer will not grasp.

Many others chose a middle road between these two

groups. In an era when Christianity was an illicit faith and Christians suffered regularly from harrassment, imprisonment, or persecution, it was to be expected that the majority would want to remain aloof from a world which frowned upon their activities. They realized, like the anonymous author of the *Epistle to Diognetus*, who perhaps wrote in this same era, that they had to live in the same cities as other men, use the same language, wear similar clothing, observe most of the same customs, and eat similar food. Yet, they did not have to strain their eyes to see that, in many respects, they set before their contemporaries a "confessedly strange character of the constitution of their own citizenship." They were strangers and sojourners in a foreign land. They did not expose unwanted infants. They displayed remarkable hospitality. They guarded their sexual purity. They went beyond obedience to the mere letter of the civil law. They were to the world, as it were, what the soul is to the body.

Diversity and Divisions

Such a picture as the last paragraph sets out is impressive, but it is much too homogenous. In actuality early Christianity incorporated people of diverse ethnic, economic, social, moral, and creedal backgrounds. When interpreted from such divergent angles, the Christian message and lifestyle came forth in a multiplicity of forms and styles.

One of the strongly debated issues in modern studies of early Christian history is the extent to which a uniform rule of faith and practice existed. The early Christian Fathers took the view that Christianity began with such a rule. Jesus delivered it to the first apostles. They delivered it to their successors. Their successors delivered it to bishops of the churches. The bishops preserved it inviolate ever after. The development of critical historical studies has made such a theory increasingly hard to believe as it stands. Consequently, modern scholars have proposed several alternatives. The most radical of these, Walter Bauer's, turned the whole question around and contended that, in the second century, there was no clear-cut or fundamental distinction between orthodoxy and heresy. Both arose simultaneously. Formal orthodoxy became dominant only gradually, particularly through the impact of the Roman church in the shaping of doctrine.

This writer tends to steer a middle road between these two extremes. He is convinced that there is a *sine qua non* which has to do with the self-disclosure of God's purpose for mankind through the life, death, and resurrection of Jesus of Nazareth. This *sine qua non* has been stated more or less closely in 1 Corinthians 15:3ff. At the same time he is convinced that what the *sine qua non* means is historically and culturally conditioned, that it depends very much upon the cultural milieu of the believer. The problem is always how far one goes beyond the center. Some in early Christianity threatened the *sine qua non* itself. In doing so, however, they helped the Church immensely to sharpen and refine its theology and, in some cases, its practice. Some of these groups deserve brief mention.

Sects and Heresies

One was the *Ebionites*, conservative Jewish Christians. There were evidently different sects of them, perhaps connected originally with the conservatives who attacked the mission of Paul to the Gentiles. They continued to observe Jewish ritual laws and regarded Jesus as a man adopted by God, filled with the divine spirit, raised from the dead, and in some sense to be regarded as Lord. After A. D. 70 they fled to Pella in Transjordan with others and existed there for a couple of centuries.

Another was the *Gnostics*, whose views were discussed in an earlier chapter. The Gnostics may have originated prior to Christianity. As associated with Christianity, however, they denied the reality of the flesh and thus Jesus' humanity. There was, of course, a profusion of Gnostic sects, but most of them viewed Jesus as a divine redeemer who appeared among men as a kind of phantom to teach *gnosis,* knowledge, from which they got their name. The *gnosis* is esoteric knowledge, the password by which one could return to heaven through the heavenly spheres guarded over by demonic powers. The leading Gnostic sect was Valentinianism, which had quite a following in Rome during the mid-second century.

A third was the *Marcionites.* Marcion was a wealthy ship-builder of Pontus on the Black Sea who was excommunicated by his own father, bishop of that church. This excommunication may have been for heresy or fornication, the source reading "defiling a virgin." At any rate he joined the Roman Church. Soon afterwards, around A. D. 140, he reacted to legalism, particularly that associated with the Old Testament, which he interpreted literally and rejected altogether. In its place he substituted Luke's Gospel and an edited version of Paul's letters. He composed a volume called *Antitheses,* contrasting the God of the Old Testament, a God of wrath and judgment, with the God revealed in Jesus, a God of love. This seems to have led him to adopt the view of a certain Gnostic teacher of Rome named Cerdo that the God of the Old Testament is a second god, a demiurge, while the God of Jesus is the Supreme God. The result was Marcion's excommunication from the Roman Church.

Not long after the Valentinian and Marcionite crises in Rome, a fourth group appeared and perhaps consolidated some trends which the Gnostics and Marcionites had set in motion. This was the *Montanists.* Montanism originated in Asia Minor, either in 156 or in 172, depending on which of two early sources one dates it from. It was essentially of a prophetic nature, called "the new prophecy" by its adherents. Its founder, a converted priest of the cult of Cybele, prophesied that the millenial reign was about to be established in his home city of Pepuza in Phrygia (Asia Minor). He believed, too, that the inspiration which he had been given fulfilled the prophecy of John 14:16, 26 concerning the Other Paraclete. He or his followers divided history into three ages:

the age of the Father (before Christ), the age of the Son, and the age of the Paraclete (from Montanus on). The dawning of the age of the Paraclete inaugurated a new discipline, which included more fasting than the churches then practiced and absolute prohibition of second marriages. Leadership depended upon the Spirit, so that women as well as men could assume places of prominence in the movement.

The Church's Reactions

Coming close on the heels of one another, Gnosticism, Marcionism, and Montanism posed severe problems for the survival of Christianity. Briefly, the churches reacted in several ways. First, they defined the confessions used in baptism and other places more closely. In Rome, for example, what is called the Old Roman Symbol took on a form relatively close to what is now known as the Apostles' Creed. It is a moot point among scholars as to what extent the Symbol developed as a reaction to Gnosticism and Marcionism. As reconstructed from contemporary documents, it consists of little more than scriptural phrases and would not have to have been *created* to answer either of those. Still, a number of items in it, for example, "the Father Almighty," directly repudiate important tenets of both Gnosticism and Marcionism.

Second, the churches compiled a canon or list of scriptures to be used in public worship. The first Christian Bible was, as is well known, the Old Testament. The Gnostics and Marcion, however, forced a decision to add to it a New Testament. In 1740 L.A. Muratori published a list, which scholars now date somewhere between 175 and 200, representing writings used by the Roman Church at the time. This list, which includes many of the writings in the present New Testament canon, was obviously designed to repudiate Marcion's canon and perhaps the tendency of Montanists to ascribe canonical authority to sayings of Montanus. The present western canon, however, did not reach its present proportions until the end of the fourth century.

Thirdly, the churches shifted teaching authority from a succession of teachers to a succession of bishops. In the first period teachers evidently accompanied missionaries wherever they went. They stayed on and continued the catechetical tasks demanded by their converts. A succession of teachers seems to have developed. The Gnostics and then others, like Justin and Clement, formed schools with evangelical designs. The existence of unlicensed and perhaps unqualified teachers, however, posed all sorts of problems. As the author of I Timothy put it: "Certain persons by swerving from these have wandered away into vain discussion, desiring to be teachers of the law, without understanding either what they are saying or the things about which they make assertions" (1 Tim. 1:6-7). The answer lay in a closer definition of teaching authority, and the persons who could best fill the bill would be the regularly constituted clergy. That, at any rate, was Ignatius's point. As he passed through Asia Minor early in the second century and found churches riddled with dissension over authenticity of doctrine, he loudly acclaimed that nothing should be done without the bishop. He did not realize yet that bishops might be heretical, but his call for a monarchical bishop who could be the focus of authority was the starting point. The bishop would become the chief teacher.

After Ignatius, who was martyred in Rome between 110 and 117, there remained the question of determining which bishops, since bishops too could disagree, to trust. The answer to that question was to turn to churches of apostolic foundation which could trace a succession of their bishops back to the apostles themselves. Irenaeus, Bishop of Lyons from about 177 to 202, framed the theory which became the underlying foundation of the catholic theory. Irenaeus indicated that he could enumerate the succession lists of several churches of apostolic foundation. For convenience' sake, however, he chose Rome and gave the list of its twelve bishops, beginning with a certain Linus, who had held the succession from the time that Peter and Paul "founded" the church. He then proceeded, in a passage whose meaning is heatedly disputed by Catholics and Protestants, to say that "every Church should agree (*convenire*) with this Church, on account of its preeminent authority (*principalitas*)." The writer has deliberately given the Latin for the two disputed words in the passage. The passage could mean, taking the two Latin words in the strongest sense, that "every Church must *conform* to (the teaching of) this Church, on account of its preeminent *authority*," or it could mean, taking the two words in the milder sense, "every Church must *agree* with (the teaching of) this Church, on account of its preeminent *antiquity*."

Finally, the churches developed a theology which they thought to be based on sounder biblical interpretation. This was, for course, no easy matter, for the Gnostics took varied approaches to the scriptures. Some rejected them entirely in favor of the "fuller" revelation which they claimed. Some rejected the Old Testament and parts of those which the Church eventually recognized as the New Testament canon, then supplemented the remainder with certain writings of their own. Most often, they employed the wildest allegorism in their interpretation, whether of Old or New Testament writings. Orthodox writers found themselves on the horns of a dilemma here, for, in their efforts to appeal to intelligent persons of Hellenistic background, they too had to move toward allegorical exposition, especially of Old Testament writings. At the same time this drew them away from the historical realities which underlay the biblical message. Usually they proceeded with caution to employ allegorical interpretation.

Christian interpretation of the primitive period is best characterized by the words literal and typological. This approach had its background in the interpretative methods of the rabbis and the Qumran community. It was based on the assumptions that every jot and tittle of scriptures are inspired and that the events of the Old Testament prefigured historically the events of the New. As Paul expressed the viewpoint in writing to the Corinthians, records of Old Testament happenings "were written down for our instruction, upon whom the end of the ages has come" (1 Cor. 10:11). Those events, according to Christian interpretation, really spoke of Christ and the Church.

~ So long as Christianity remained largely within the Jewish matrix, which it did for a generation or two, typological interpretation sufficed. When it ventured farther and farther into the Hellenistic world, however, the message of the scriptures gave off an alien sound. The historical orientation which was entirely intelligible to Jews was not intelligible to Gentiles. Therefore, the Gnostics and some of the orthodox Fathers shifted from an essentially historical to a more cosmological approach to the scriptures. Philo, the great Jewish apologist of Alexandria, had already done that for the Pentateuch. Now Christians began to do it for the prophetic writings of the Old Testament and even the gradually growing list of writings which became the New Testament.

Before A. D. 200 orthodox writers employed the allegorical method with obvious caution. Paul dabbled in it slightly, for example, in the Sarah-Hagar story of Galatians 3. As observed earlier, Mark allegorized the parable of the sower. A late-first or early-second century writer who used the name of Barnabas went a bit further than earlier persons to expound a rationale for allegorization of Old Testament liturgical customs. Justin stayed rather close to typology. Irenaeus, responding to the wild speculations of Gnostics which they read into the scriptures, repudiated the allegorical method while employing it fairly extensively himself. It was in Alexandria that the boldest use of allegory occurred. Against the background of Philo's work first Clement and, during the third century, Origen rivaled the Gnostics for allegorical interpretation. Neither of these, however, ever lost sight of the historical actualities which underlay the scriptures, and it was that which steered their interpretation away from the reefs which sank the Gnostics. By their method the Gnostics could find in the scriptures anything which they wanted to find there or explain away anything they wanted to explain away. Clement and Origen could do both to some degree, but they at least anchored their thought loosely in the historical realities underlying the scriptures with which they dealt.

Holy Church

As it penetrated the alien and often hostile Hellenistic world, early Christianity envisioned itself as the People of Light engaged in the struggle of the end time with the People of Darkness. Most Christians expected the consummation to occur soon, but they realized as time passed that it would not occur as soon as the first apostles may have expected. Meantime, the ranks grew. As they grew, Christianity developed institutionally in ways which require brief description.

Initiation

In the primitive period converts from Judaism were initiated by baptism with little catechetical instruction. The conversion of Gentiles who had had little previous contact with the doctrine and ways of Judaism, however, revealed quickly the need for more careful formation. What began as a simple process became by the early third century a careful formation process lasting up to three years in some churches and entailing at least four and possibly five stages.

The first stage involved a preliminary sketch of Christian doctrine and an examination of the applicant's motives for wanting to become a Christian. How soon this procedure began is uncertain. It was clearly fixed when Hippolytus wrote the *Apostolic Tradition*, around 215, and possibly was the procedure for which Irenaeus composed *The Proof of the Apostolic Teaching*. According to Hippolytus, applicants in certain professions were required to change jobs, and magicians, as pawns of the Devil, were rejected altogether. The churches had obviously been stung by certain persons who came for unsound motives and with inadequate sense of commitment.

The second stage involved lengthy catechetical instruction. Scholars have long debated when pre-baptismal instruction of this type first began. *The Teaching of the Twelve Apostles*, probably composed by about A. D. 100, required some preliminary teaching. The writer would judge that such instruction, however brief, occurred almost as soon as the churches incorporated large numbers of Gentiles. At any rate Hippolytus required up to three years of instruction depending upon the progress of the convert in the rudiments of Christian behavior. One early document required as many as six years!

The third stage represented the final spiritual preparation before the actual baptism. This began as a period of fasting two days prior to baptism, but it too elongated until, by the fourth century, it involved the present Lenten season before Easter. Besides fasting, it included special prayers, exorcisms, laying-on-of-hands, and such other things as would equip the candidate for his battle with the forces of evil after baptism.

The fourth stage, baptism itself, went from simple immersion to an impressive, dramatic rite which symbolized the departure from the kingdom of Satan and entrance into the kingdom of Christ. At one time the rite may have taken place without regard to the calendar, but by the end of the second century it was the custom to baptize on Easter Sunday morning at sunrise or, exceptionally, on Pentecost. As described by Hippolytus, the rite had the following form:

Prayer over the water to invoke the Holy Spirit to sanctify and empower it.

Removal of clothing and other apparel for nude baptism.

Blessing of the "oil of thanksgiving" by the bishop.

Blessing of the "oil of exorcism."

Renunciation of "Satan, his pomp and his service" by the baptizand, facing West.

Anointing with the oil of exorcism (over the entire body) by a presbyter.

Acknowledgment of Christ or of the Trinity by the baptizand, facing East.

Threefold immersion upon confession of Father, Son, and Holy Spirit.

Anointing with the oil of thanksgiving (over the entire body) by a presbyter.

Reclothing and entering the assembly.

(Footwashing in some churches.)

Laying-on-of-hands by the bishop, invoking the grace of the Holy Spirit.

Anointing with consecrated oil, sealing on the forehead, and giving the kiss of peace by the bishop.

Prayers with the whole assembly and exchanging the kiss of peace.

Observance of the eucharist, including in some instances the giving of milk and honey.

A fifth stage was added later. It began evidently with a brief explanation of the meaning of baptism and the first communion, mentioned by Hippolytus, immediately after baptism. By the fourth century this had been lengthened to a week of instruction in the "mysteries" after baptism.

Worship

It was to be expected that Christian worship, like initiation, would evolve as Christianity kept expanding in the Hellenistic world. One aspect of this evolution involved the liturgy itself, a second the meaning of the eucharist as the central rite of Christian worship, and a third the development of a calendar and other aids to worship.

In the primitive period, as the writer recorded earlier, Christians engaged in several types of worship. As the Christian movement became increasingly detached from Judaism, however, strictly Jewish forms — temple and synagogue worship — gave way to forms which were more distinctively Christian. By the early second century what is now called the Lord's Supper had become detached from the fellowship meal (*agápe*) and had become attached to the Lord's Day liturgy, which resembled the Jewish synagogue liturgy. In the mid-second century Justin reported the following liturgy:

> Reading of the "memoirs of the apostles" or the writings of the prophets "as long as time permits."
>
> Verbal instruction by the "president" (bishop?) and exhortation "to the imitation of these good things."
>
> Prayer with all standing.
>
> Presentation of bread and wine mixed with water along with other oblations.
>
> Prayers and thanksgiving offered by the "president" "according to his ability."
>
> "Amen!" by the congregation.
>
> Distribution of the bread and water-wine by the deacons.
>
> Delivering of the remaining portions along with other oblations by the deacons.
>
> Collection of money with the "president" for the care of orphans, widows, the sick, the imprisoned, and strangers.

How the eucharist became detached from the *Agápe* meal and attached to the Sunday liturgy is a subject of much interest but cannot be pursued here. Two other matters should be mentioned, however. One is the fact that, from a very early time, certainly by the end of the first century (*Didache* 9.5), participation in the eucharist was denied the unbaptized. This custom led, possibly during the second century, to the practice of dismissing catechumens after the sermon. By the fourth century the liturgy had two clearly delineated parts — the liturgy for the catechumens and the liturgy for believers. Another is the addition of certain other elements to the liturgy such as the preface ("The Lord be with you," etc.), the eucharistic thanksgiving, and other prayers.

As a peculiarly Christian rite, it was natural that the Lord's Supper or eucharist would be reinterpreted as Christianity moved from the Jewish to the Hellenistic setting. The reinterpretation proceeded along two lines suggested by the views of the earliest Christian communities.

One of these was *sacrifice.* No primitive Christian writer, of course, spoke directly of the eucharist as a sacrifice, but the Apostle Paul came very close to that when he warned the Corinthians, "You cannot partake of the table of the Lord and the table of demons" (1 Cor. 10:21). In his letter to the Corinthians, written about A. D. 96, Clement of Rome applied Old Testament sacrificial language rather freely to describe the Christian liturgy. The Christian apologists, subsequently, did not hesitate to speak of the eucharist as the "bloodless sacrifice" of Christianity which supplanted the "carnal sacrifices" of the pagan cults or of Judaism. Irenaeus could call the eucharist "the oblation of the Church," "the new oblation of the new covenant," "the first-fruits of [God's] own created things," and "the pure sacrifice."

The other was that of *the real presence.* From the beginning Christians thought of a real presence of Christ in relationship to the Lord's Supper. If Willy Rordorf is correct, they called the first day of the week the "Lord's day" because it was on that day that they first experienced his presence at table among them. In the post-apostolic period this concept of the real presence remained and, indeed, was strengthened with a realism and perhaps materialism which went beyond the earliest interpretations, almost certainly as a consequence of the Gnostic rejection of Christ's real humanity. The eucharist became the symbol par excellence of his real humanity. Thus John, alluding to the eucharist in connection with the feeding of the five thousand, spoke in starkly realistic terms of "eating the flesh" and "drinking the blood" as requirements for participation in his life (John 6:35). Ignatius equated the bread with Christ's "flesh" and identified the eucharist as "the medicine of immortality, the antidote that we should not die, but live forever in Jesus Christ" (Eph. 20:2). A generation later Justin explained how, by invocation of the words of institution over bread and wine, the latter are transmuted into "the flesh and blood of that Jesus who was made flesh." By receiving the transmuted bread and wine, according to Irenaeus, the bodies of believers "are no longer corruptible, having the hope of the resurrection to eternity" (*Against Heresies*, 4.18.5). The eucharist fortified the recipient against all of the assaults of evil.

Developments in the liturgy and in understanding of the eucharist were accompanied by the development of a Christian calendar. Christianity inherited from Judaism some appreciation for a calendar. This was due to the fact that, in both religions, revelation was believed to be connected with historical events. As in other customs, however, Christianity sometimes accepted and sometimes repudiated what it received from its parent. Christian calendar observances, therefore, were essentially new, commemorations of great moments in the history of salvation connected especially with Christ.

The first Christian special day was probably *the "Lord's day,"* observed as a day of worship on the first day of the week in honor of Jesus' resurrection. At first probably it began, according to Jewish custom, at six in the evening on the Jewish sabbath or Saturday. By the early second century it had shifted to the Roman Sunday, beginning at sunrise on the first day of the week. Christians hesitated to use the name Sunday, since it commemorated the pagan Sun-God, and they did not think of it as a day of rest. The day did not become a legal holiday until Constantine made it that in 321.

Almost from the beginning Christians *fasted.* According to the *Teaching of the Twelve Apostles*, by the late first century they chose Wednesdays and Fridays to contrast with Jewish fast days on Tuesdays and Thursdays.

The first annual calendar observance of Christians was *Easter.* A controversy over the date of observance in the second century proves that it had become a universal custom by that time. As an observance, it entailed the breaking of a fast of two days duration. Christians in Asia Minor broke the fast in accordance with the Jewish Passover.

Elsewhere, however, they broke the fast on Sunday after the first full moon after the spring equinox, the present custom of celebrating Jesus' resurrection. It was not until the

Council of Nicaea in 325, however, that consensus was reached for Christians of both Asia Minor and Rome; even then, some easterners refused to accept the decision.

The second annual calendar observance was probably *Pentecost*. Like the other observances, it too had Jewish roots. As the name *Pentecost* implied in Greek, it occurred on the "fiftieth" day after Passover and recalled the beginning of the harvest, the offering of "first fruits" in the Temple. Among Christians, however, it referred to the outpouring of the Spirit and the beginnings of the Church.

In Alexandria in Egypt there may have been some observance of the birth of Christ during the second century, but the evidence for this is flimsy. Later on, eastern Christians celebrated the birth on January 6. The current custom of remembering Christ's birth on December 25 originated in the West during the time of Constantine, perhaps around 335. That date was connected with a pagan festival in honor of the Unconquered Sun.

Besides the calendar, other aids to worship also developed during the second century. Alongside Hebrew-type hymnody, based chiefly on parallelism, metrical songs in Greek, Syriac, and possibly even Latin began to augment the Sunday worship. Christian art began to develop, first from lay interest and customarily with opposition from the clergy. This art, best seen in the catacombs, combined the decadent art of the late Roman period with Christian symbolism. Buildings specially designed for the purposes of worship were not feasible in a time of persecution. Christians met in homes. Later on, some homes were remodeled so as to serve the functions of worship better. A house-church of this type, dating from A. D. 232, was discovered at Dura-Europos. It had three rooms, one to accommodate about a hundred worshippers, a second for the communal meal, and a third which served as a baptistry.

Pastoral Care

Early Christianity's ambitious goal of winning all and sundry was bound in time to generate problems in pastoral discipline. Already in the primitive period serious lapses occurred, showing that some failed not merely in practice but even in comprehension of the Christian life. In later generations, too, there were Ananiases and Sapphiras, Simon Maguses, and many like them. A certain Gnostic named Marcus seduced gullible women. A charlatan named Alexander preyed on simple Christians to get money. It is perhaps less surprising that Christianity had such lapses than that it had no more than it did, for, unlike many competitors, it had an open door policy regarding membership.

How were these cases requiring discipline handled? For many years Protestants took the view that the earliest Church held a very rigorous and strict policy and that the later Church let it slip. The main evidence for this view has been the exceedingly harsh attack which Hippolytus of Rome made on his contemporary Callistus and which Tertullian made on the "pontifex maximus," whom many have identified with Callistus also. Objective evaluation of the evidence shows that this long and strongly held view cannot stand. Instead, from the beginning there were both rigorists and laxists in the early Church. The question was always how discipline should be applied.

On the rigorist side, the author of the early second century writing called the Shepherd of Hermas knew some Roman teachers who would allow no repentance for persons who committed serious sins. Hermas did not define what sins these teachers would have included, but they would presumably have included apostasy, adultery, and murder — the mortal sins of later writings. Tertullian and Hippolytus were representatives of the same view. As a matter of fact, Tertullian probably became a Montanist because the Montanists held similarly rigorous views, for his own Catholic writings prove that at one time he would have allowed anyone to be restored to the Church after proper repentance.

On the opposite side, which could not really be called lenient in the modern day, some viewed the Church as a mixed body and allowed restoration of all or most offenders. Matthew evidently reflected such a view in his parable of the wheat and the tares. Callistus of Rome did so also as he urged restoration of persons who repented the sin of fornication or impurity.

Hermas himself seems to have wanted to adopt a mediating position. At any rate his decision to allow one repentance after baptism was by no means a lenient one, but it was a decision which influenced Christian discipline for centuries. Hermas realized that serious Christians might slip, but he did not want to leave the door wide open to frequent lapses.

It became evident in time that the crucial issue was authenticity of an offender's repentance. In the primitive period the apostles had required modest displays of remorse and extended ready forgiveness (2 Cor. 2:5ff.). But persons who lack self-discipline could display remorse and then return in a thrice to old habits. To avoid embarrassments from critical outsiders and to aid genuine restoration, the churches developed more self-evident means for manifesting real repentance. This "confessional" involved several steps: After exclusion from the fellowship the penitent donned sordid garb, sackcloth and ashes, fasted for a time, displayed public lamentation, prostrated himself before the elders of the church, and kneeled before the congregation. The congregation then interceded with the elders to restore him if they thought he had done adequate "penance." Obviously anyone who had gone through such a grueling display would think twice about committing a similar offense.

Structures

As Christianity expanded little by little, it was inevitable that it would expand its structures. Old structures grow and new ones spring up for various reasons. For Christianity, however, a dominant reason was the need for leadership created by the expansion itself. Although no modern historian can naively agree with the ancient theory that the apos-

tles planted churches and appointed successors and then the
latter appointed others to succeed them and so on *ad infini-
tum*, there is a certain truth bound up with that view. The
truth is that a process of structuring did have to take place, and
this process led to the Church as seen at the end of the second
century.

The development of ecclesiastical structures has to be ex-
amined both at the local and on the universal level. This is
not to say, as Adolf Harnack once argued, that Christianity
had two separate structures, one for local communities and
the other for the Church universal. On the contrary, the
whole Church, the Body of Christ, had an organic unity
which extended to local communities. The term *ecclesia*, in
fact, could be used to designate either the local or the universal reality. For the sake of clarity, however, the writer will
speak first of local organization and then discuss ecumenical
ties.

The term Church designated locally all Christians living in
a city, the Greek *polis*, however many congregations that
might have included. Churches planted in these cities, however, tended to extend their mission work beyond the confines of the city to include the surrounding area. Thus, in the
early second century, Ignatius could speak of himself both as
bishop of Antioch and bishop of Syria. To all intents and
purposes, the diocese was already being formed.

Around A. D. 70 the common structure for most local
churches was bi-partite — presbyter-bishops and deacons.
The Greek term translated bishop, *episkopos*, most scholars
now believe, was a functional term which described the work
of the presbyter. The office of presbyter was one which the
Church inherited from the synagogue. Every local community of Christians, like every synagogue, had a plurality of
presbyter-bishops, who, as the name *episkopos* implies, were
responsible for the overall administration, the superintending
of the various local congregations. They preached, taught,
presided at the eucharist, baptized, performed marriages,

and did a myriad other jobs. One of them possibly served as "presiding" presbyter.

The office of deacon had no exact prototype in the synagogue, although some scholars have seen parallels to the *hazzan*, the paid synagogue attendant. The term meant minister, and from the first the deacon assisted the presbyter-bishops at baptism, in worship, and in distributing the charities. These functions changed little during the early centuries.

During the second century, most local churches shifted from a bi-partite to a tri-partite structure and the monarchical episcopate emerged. As indicated earlier, James functioned as a kind of monarchical bishop in Jerusalem until his death in A. D. 64. So far as one can determine from the evidence, however, few other churches, had an analogous pattern. It surfaced with Ignatius of Antioch during the early second century. As indicated above, Ignatius denominated himself bishop of Antioch and Syria. Moreover, as he traveled around Asia Minor, he touted the authority of the bishop as a solution to the threat of heresy in the churches to which he wrote his letters. Two bits of evidence, however, indicate that not all of the churches to which Ignatius wrote actually had the monarchical episcopate. One is the fact that he had to acclaim the office so loudly and so contentiously. Had the episcopate been well established, he would not have needed to have said again and again, "Do nothing without the bishop!" Indeed, he felt compelled in one letter to claim inspiration of the Spirit for the whole idea. The other is the fact that, in his letter to Rome, Ignatius did not name a bishop, which suggests perhaps that, as of this date, Rome did not have the monarchical episcopate. It would seem to be a terribly serious omission for one as interested in the episcopate as he that he failed to allude at all to a Roman bishop if there was one. The bi-partite pattern seems to have prevailed in Rome until after the middle of the second century.

What caused the shift from the bi-partite to the tri-partite structure? Protestants have long emphasized the threat of heresy which confronted the churches of Asia Minor when Ignatius wrote, and that threat was obviously a factor in accelerating a process. The historian must ask, however, whether an earlier crisis was not at work, particularly in Antioch, where the monarchical episcopate was to emerge first. An Anglican scholar has suggested that the death of James and the leadership vacuum left by the Fall of Jerusalem presented just such a crisis. Antioch replaced Jerusalem in the place of leadership, and Ignatius's predecessor replaced James. The true answer may never be known.

Although the cause remains obscure, it is possible to suggest how the shift occurred. In the bi-partite structure one of the presbyters almost certainly functioned as a chairman of the board of presbyters, the *presbyterion*. J. B. Lightfoot suggested long ago that the chairman gradually assumed more authority. The name bishop was then reserved for him alone and the name presbyter applied to other members of the board. The increase of the bishop's authority could have occurred in the natural process of evolution, perhaps accelerated by crises of one sort or another but not created by them.

The tri-partite structure was more or less standard everywhere by the end of the second century. Various regions differed, however, in number of episcopates. Asia Minor, Palestine, and North Africa had monarchical bishops in almost every city. Italy, Gaul, and Egypt had few episcopates, so that presbyters and even deacons functioned in capacities usually reserved for bishops in the other areas. In 177 Irenaeus was made bishop of Lyons, but his territory covered all of Gaul and even Germany. By 250 Italy still had only seven bishops. At the same time Dionysius of Alexandria thought of all Egypt as his responsibility.

At the end of the period under discussion the broader structures were not clearly defined. As Christianity spread from the cities to outlying areas, it left many blurred edges regarding pastoral and missionary responsibility. Some cities held special eminence by virtue of their part in the beginnings and spread of Christianity — Jerusalem, Antioch, Ephesus, Rome, Alexandria, and Carthage. The work, however, was still too vast and Christianity's survival still too much at stake to leave time for squabbling over jurisdiction. Such matters waited for the conversion of Constantine and the flood of new converts which accompanied it.

A. D. 200

By the year 200 Christianity had come of age in the Roman Empire. Tertullian boasted, perhaps not inaccurately, that the Christian witness reached every city, village, and hamlet in and around the Empire. Christianity was being noticed, too, in the upper ranks of society. It had largely overcome a once-sordid reputation. Growth, however, had brought pains as well as pleasures. The varied peoples who attached themselves to the Church interpreted and applied their faith in a variety of ways. Sects appeared. The influx of an increasing number of Gentiles necessitated more careful procedures in initiation. It brought changes in worship. It posed problems of pastoral discipline not faced earlier. It forced the expansion of structures. In A. D. 200 Christianity was showing essentially the form it would have throughout the period of the Fathers.

Epilogue:
Trial, Triumph
and Twilight

The final period of history with which this volume will deal can be discussed only in a very sketchy manner. The writer feels that this is unfortunate, for his own (free church) tradition has tended to neglect and even to denigrate the period as the time of the Church's "fall," particularly after Constantine. The writer's own perception of the period is more positive, for, alongside developments which did perhaps threaten and obscure the true character of Christianity, many positive developments occurred. Perhaps the event which stands out among the others was the fact that Christianity survived two highly concerted efforts to wipe it out and then became the chosen religion of the Empire.

Christianity's institutional outlines were sufficiently set by the beginning of this period, A. D. 200 to 400, that the writer will not consume precious space by describing them further. Here rather, he will concentrate upon the relationships between Christianity and the Empire which improved so dramatically and radically in the fourth century, the schisms and heresies which arose during this time, and monasticism, the development which was to have the most significant repercussions for the future as twilight fell in the West.

Christ and Caesar
The relationship between Christianity and the Roman state

was not entirely one of confrontation during the period before Constantine and Licinius issued the Edict of Milan in 313. Periods of peace were mingled with periods of intensive repression. The era under discussion, however, differed from the preceding one chiefly in that the state became more and more conscious that Christianity's demand of absolute allegiance posed a threat to the state's demand of absolute allegiance. It is not strange at all, then, that the persecuting emperors in this era were not the weak, bumbling rulers but the strong ones who were intent on revivifying a sagging internal morale as well as halting the advance of enemies from outside.

The Final Onslaught

The first deliberate, intensive, organized persecution occurred under Decius, a field general of considerable experience and sagacity. In A. D. 250 he issued an edict which demanded that all Christians in town and country secure certificates of sacrifice. The penalty for failure to do so by a set date was exile with confiscation of property. The authorities did not hesitate to employ torture and imprisonment to induce compliance, but they seldom inflicted the death penalty. The persecution was universal. It aimed particularly at leaders. As a result, many bishops, including Fabian of Rome, were its victims. Fortunately, Decius died in battle on the Gallic front before the persecution gained too much momentum.

Decius' immediate successor, Gallus, issued a new edict requiring Christians to make the prescribed sacrifice. The next emperor, Valerian, however, halted the persecution for a few years (253-257) and then reinstituted it with new edicts. The first of these ordered bishops and presbyters to worship the gods under penalty of death and forbade Christians to frequent the cemetaries or hold assemblies for worship. A second, in 258, commanded that bishops, presbyters, and deacons who refused to sacrifice should be put to death at once; that Christians of noble birth should have their property confiscated; and that people of lower station should lose their property and be made slaves of the soil. The most distinguished martyrs were Sixtus II of Rome and Cyprian of Carthage.

The severe policy toward Christianity was alleviated when Gallienus succeeded Valerian in 260. Gallienus, whom some scholars have thought had Christian leanings, granted toleration by way of permitting use of the cemetaries and places of worship. There were isolated cases of persecution, but nothing consequential for the Church as a whole. Gallienus's successor, Aurelian, issued a new edict against Christianity, but died before it could be executed. Thus for a period of roughly forty years Christianity had peace. Meantime, it expanded rapidly, being able even to build some special houses for worship. It would appear that the emperors were beginning to recognize the endurance if not the value of Christianity as one of the religions of the Empire.

The persecution which suddenly burst forth in 303 under Diocletian and Maximian, therefore, came as a major surprise, and it was perhaps the most severe, certainly the most shaking of all the persecutions. After purging the army, in 303 Diocletian issued the first edict, which ordered churches destroyed, scriptures burned, Christians holding high offices degraded, and Christians of low rank enslaved. The edict did not prescribe the death penalty, but many persons died. A second edict ordered Christian leaders jailed. A third ordered that clergy who refused to offer the public sacrifice should suffer the most cruel tortures. A fourth, in 304, commanded all Christians to offer the sacrifice or be put to death. The persecution had become a war of extermination.

This persecution continued intermittently under the successors of Diocletian and Maximian until the Emperor Galerius, on his deathbed, issued the *Palinode*, an edict of toleration designed to obtain Christian prayers for him in his extremity. Galerius' co-emperor, Maximin Daza, however, went on with the persecution after the death of Galerius.

Toleration finally came in March 313 when Constantine and Licinius, after the victory at the Milvian Bridge, issued the famous Edict of Milan. This Edict gave Christianity the same legal status granted other religions of the Empire. All Christians, the Edict read, are "to be permitted to continue therein, without any let or hindrance, and are not to be in any way troubled or molested."

Christianity as the Favored Religion

Here was a charter for genuine religious liberty. Unfortunately it did not last, for Constantine soon showed that he favored Christianity over all the other religions of the Empire. Save for the reign of Julian (361-3), favoritism to Christianity grew steadily for a century. Under Theodosius I (379-395) Christianity became the established religion of the Empire.

The intriguing question here is: Why did Constantine halt the persecution and adopt Christianity? It would not be wise to place too much of the burden of explanation upon the famous story of Constantine's vision before the battle at the Milvian bridge, but that incident should not be totally discounted. Constantine, whatever else he was, was a superstitious person who believed in signs, auguries, and portents. The fact that he and Licinius won would have reinforced whatever he thought the Christian God communicated to him in the sign. Another factor, however, was surely the recognition that Christianity had by this time become such a potent and sizeable force in the Empire that it could not be easily stamped out. By this time Christians composed ten to fifteen percent of the population of the Empire. In some areas they comprised at least half the population. In addition, Christianity showed itself to have a powerful cohesive effect. It held together peoples of varied ethnic, social, intellectual, economic, and other backgrounds in a worldwide organization matched only by the administration of the Empire itself.

Constantine, by all accounts, was not a brilliant person,

but he could not have failed to see that Christianity represented a religion which would hold together the vast, far-flung Empire which he governed. As a Roman, he would have believed strongly that the right religion, rightly observed, had much to do with the destiny of the Empire. Religiously he had two choices. One, he could go along with the solar monotheism which had been growing since the second century and was centered especially in the cult of Mithra. Some of his predecessors, like Commodus (180-192), had opted for Mithra. Two, he could chose Christianity, which had an even stronger monotheism, but much more, an organizational unity which the solar monotheism of Mithra could not equal: In the end, he opted for Christianity. It was not at all remarkable that, a few years later, he entered with elan into issues bearing upon Christian unity.

Constantine did not play his full hand all at once. He proceeded little by little to put Christianity into a more favorable position. As Andreas Alföldi has pointed out, from 312 to 320 he hardly touched paganism, but he elevated the standing of the Church "with increasing energy." He restored church buildings destroyed by his predecessors, granted special favors to the clergy, and built grand new houses of worship in various parts of the Empire. From 320 to 330 he thrust the organization of the Church into the foreground of public life and directed a frontal attack on polytheism. Then, in 330, he moved his capital from Rome to Byzantium, Constantinople, and waged an open war on the old religion, probably discouraged at the tenacity of the state cultus in ancient Rome, especially among the aristocracy.

To some persons, like Eusebius of Caesarea, the great church historian, Constantine's accession seemed like the beginning of the millenium. Constantine himself, according to Eusebius, had a placard erected in front of his palace on which he pictured himself and his sons with feet perched atop a huge serpent into which they were casting daggers. Satan, "that old serpent," was at last cast down.

Constantine's successors, too, excepting Julian, seemed to carry the victory on toward its ultimate fruition. Vast numbers flocked to the churches. The climax came with Theodosius' decree proscribing all religions except Christianity. As it turned out, however, this favoritism was not entirely fortuitous. The influx of new converts created unparalleled problems of discipline and of doctrine. Theological splits rent the churches asunder. Many of the most devout turned their backs upon the burgeoning institution and chose solitary forms of spirituality. To some it may have seemed that Satan had fallen but had taken up his residence *inside* the Church rather than outside.

Schisms and Heresies

As in both of its earlier periods, Christianity again experienced the agony of divisions. This time, they involved greater numbers, in large part because Christianity had grown a great deal. This time, too, they had to do much more with fine distinctions in theology than they had earlier, because the new converts had better cultural and educational preparation than earlier generations and were more diverse than ever.

The divisions are usually distinguished in two groups, schisms and heresies. Schisms normally did not involve theological points, heresies normally did. However, it is not difficult to perceive that distinctions between theological and non-theological are somewhat artificial and that different interpreters might view a particular movement now as heresy, now as schism. In this instance, generally speaking, the schisms preceded and the heresies followed Constantine's conversion. That strange fact is perhaps due to the fact that the Constantinian settlement allowed more leisure for theological reflection than the previous era.

Schisms

Schisms were numerous throughout this period, but only two involved sufficient numbers to merit consideration here.

Both of these occurred chiefly as a result of disagreements over the disciplining of persons who lapsed during persecution. As the writer indicated in the preceding chapter, the Church had probably had "rigorists" and "laxists" from the beginning. On the issue of apostasy most Christians were in agreement that deliberate, blatant returners to paganism merited little consideration with reference to restoration to the Church and, no doubt, seldom sought restoration through public confession. What divided them was whether denial of their faith under torture or severe threat of torture constituted apostasy. Both the Decian and the Diocletianic persecutions put this issue to the test and resulted in schisms. In each instance, however, other complex factors entered the picture.

The schism which occurred as a result of the Decian persecution was associated with a Roman presbyter named Novatian, one of the two chief candidates to succeed Bishop Fabian, martyred in 251. Although Novatian had offered decisive leadership after Fabian's death, the Roman people did not vote decisively for him when an election was finally held. Instead, they split their vote between him and Cornelius, another presbyter. There is strong reason to suspect that the lack of support was due to Novatian's rigorist views, but the records leave no clear statement on the matter. At any rate, the Romans appealed to three other bishops — Dionysius of Alexandria, Fabian of Antioch, and Cyprian of Carthage — to help them reach a decision. Fabian voted for Novatian, Dionysius for Cornelius. Cyprian waited three months and then, to everyone's surprise since Novatian had assisted him in his reinstatement as bishop of Carthage, cast his vote for Cornelius also. A disaffected deacon of Carthage named Novatus wrote to Novatian and counseled him to form a separate Church. He did.

The Novatianist schism lasted for several centuries. During the fourth century Arian dispute, Catholics welcomed Novatianist support of the Nicene creed. In 412, however, the Emperor Honorius issued a severe edict against them. By the sixth century most of their churches had been merged with the Catholic Church or had died out. They differed solely on the matter of discipline, not on doctrine.

The schism which resulted from the persecution under Diocletian was limited to North Africa. The roots of it went back to an attitude which Cyprian of Carthage held toward the restoration of schismatics, especially the Novatianists. His view was that Novatianists as well as heretics should be rebaptized before readmission to the Catholic Church. This attitude conflicted with that of Stephen, Bishop of Rome who restored penitent Novatianists and even Marcionites by laying-on-of-hands only. A rift between the two was probably obviated by the martyrdom of Cyprian in 258.

The issue which the Diocletianic persecution posed was the validity of rites — baptism, eucharist, ordination — performed by persons who had surrendered copies of scripture during the persecution, which some considered apostasy, or had received baptism or ordination by such persons. This issue was first posed in 311 at the ordination of a certain Caecilian as bishop of Carthage, for Caecilian was accused of surrendering copies of scripture and of being consecrated by another bishop, Felix of Aptunga, charged with the same crime. Caecilian's opponents appealed to Constantine to referee the disputed consecration. When a commission appointed by Constantine and then the Council of Arles decided in favor of Caecilian, the disputing party formed a new sect. Later the sect took the name of Donatus, one of the later leaders of it.

Like Novatianism, Donatism too involved chiefly a concern for discipline. Its view of ecclesiastical rites, however, did pose theological issues of some significance which occupied the best theologian the West produced in the fourth century, Augustine of Hippo, for several years. The Donatists operated on the theory that the Church is made pure by the purity of its individual members. If one member is bad, he defiles the whole Body. The Catholic Church's toleration of persons guilty of surrendering copies of scripture in persecution, therefore, the Donatists argued, had resulted in its total corruption. As a corrupted Church, it could not perform valid sacraments, for the validity of a sacrament depends upon the purity of the administrator. Thus Donatists rebaptized Catholics and reordained Catholic clergy.

Behind the Donatist argument there was a valid concern, that is, for a worthy ministry. Theologically, however, they overlooked some issues which weakened their movement and left it vulnerable in the long run. The chief issue was whether the Church's purity can ever depend upon the purity of individual members. As Augustine pointed out, such a claim, even among the Donatists, falls down in the face of the facts. The Church is always a mixed body as regards its individual members.Whatever purity the Church may claim will always depend upon Christ, therefore, not upon the individual members of his Body. If this is true, then what the Church does will also depend for its validity upon Christ. Here Augustine distinguished between the validity and the efficacy of sacraments. Sacraments are valid because of Christ alone. The purity of the administrator cannot affect their validity. They do not become effective for salvation, however, unless the recipient appropriates them by faith.

Donatism, although confined always to North Africa, thrived for about a century. Near the end of the fourth century Donatist churches numerically equalled Catholic churches in North Africa. Several things turned the tide against them, however. One was their inability to produce a spokesman for Donatist theology of the caliber of Augustine. Indeed, they excommunicated the one person, named Tyconius, who might put together a sound expression of their concern for a worthy ministry. A second was their use of violence against Catholics. At least one party of them, the Circumcellions, carried on a kind of guerilla warfare, defacing Catholic churches, beating the clergy, and wreaking havoc on individuals. A third, perhaps in great part prompted by reaction to Donatist violence, was imperial suppression from 406 on. The use of coercion was sustained, reluctantly, by Augustine himself. His argument for it, unfortunately, became the foundation upon which the Inquisition of the Middle Ages was founded: Love should compel the erring to come in!

Heresies

Like divisions regarding ecclesiastical practices, divisions regarding theological matters did not crop up for the first time during the third and fourth centuries. Indeed, it is a moot issue, as discussed earlier, whether heresy or orthodoxy came first. By A. D. 200, nevertheless, clearer lines for discriminating between heresy and orthodoxy were being laid out, especially, as Harnack said, in canon, creed, and episcopacy. Still the tumultuous and often threatening third century did not allow Christians to develop their theology as much as they might have had there been a more favorable situation. The two notable exceptions were Tertullian, who, however, turned Montanist about 206, and Origen.

Against the Gnostics, Marcion, and a group called modalists or Sabellians, Tertullian formulated no systematic theology, but he did frame important christological statements which helped the West to avoid some of the heated controversies which rent the eastern churches in the fourth century. One of these concerned the relation of Christ as the divine Logos or Son to the Father. Sabellians or modalists solved this problem by saying that God is *successively* Father, Son, and Spirit. At one time He operated in the *mode* of the Father (before the incarnation), at another time in the *mode* of the Son, and at a third time in the *mode* of the Spirit (after the ascension of Jesus). Tertullian contended, to the contrary, that God is *simultaneously* Father, Son, and Spirit. He functions at one and the same time in all three *modes*. One can say, therefore, that there is "one entity (*substantia*) in three persons (*personae*)." This would be analogous to a single individual functioning at the same time in the roles of father, son, and husband or three persons forming a single corporation.

Tertullian also anticipated the subsequent discussion of the relation between the human and divine natures in the incarnation. He denied a fusion or mixing of the natures so as to form a *tertium quid*, that is, an alloy of some kind.

Like Tertullian, Origen too was not a systematic theologian, although he did compose, as a young man, Christianity's first systematic theology. He was really a biblical exegete, and he spent much of his life composing homilies and commentaries on the scriptures. In his allegorical excursions with the scriptures, however, the brilliant Alexandrian touched on nearly every point of theology and left later generations pondering a multitude of questions. Prolific writer that he was, it was his misfortune to be quoted on both sides of nearly every issue in the theological debates of the fourth century. The writer cannot give here an extended statement of Origen's christology, which later became an object of contention, but it is necessary to point out that the chief issue is how he saw the Son's subordination to the Father. Did he teach a subordination of *essence*, as Arius held, or a subordination of *function*, as orthodox theology would allow? Depending on which writing one cites, both views may be sustainable. Like most easterners, Origen was greatly concerned to differentiate clearly between Father and Son lest, as in Sabellianism, the Son's redemptive role be confused and compromised. In a recently rediscovered work describing Origen's debate with a certain Heracleides, Origen strove mightily to prove from the scriptures that Christ is a "second God," a view adopted also by Justin during the second century but with much less exegetical and theological acumen. The point was, the Son had to be altogether distinct from the Father, so that a true union between him and individual humanity could occur. Depending on how far Origen was willing to stress the point, he could have implied a distinction of essence or nature as well as of function.

Arius, at least feigning fear of Sabellianism, interpreted Origen as teaching the former. Behind his thought, however, lay another tradition rooted more in the Palestinian soil of Antioch. This christology emphasized Christ's human nature on the basis of more literal exegesis of scripture and tended to think along lines similiar to the old Ebionites, that is, that Christ was adopted as God's Son. A certain Paul of Samosata was condemned in 268 by a synod of bishops as an adoptionist. But it was from Paul's pupil, Lucian of Antioch, that Arius borrowed his idea that the Logos or Son which became incarnate in Jesus was created.

The Arian controversy began in 318 when Arius, who had taken a church in Alexandria, accused the Bishop of Alexandria, Alexander, of the Sabellian heresy. Alexander reciprocated by convening a synod of clergy which declared Arius' views heretical and exiled him from Alexandria. Arius gathered support among Palestinians and the East was soon in an uproar over the issue of the Son's relation to the Father. The Emperor Constantine, jarred by witnessing the smashing of an ardently desired unitive force throughout the Empire, followed the advice of Hosius, Bishop of Cordova, Spain, in calling a universal council at Nicaea, not far from Constantinople, in 325.

The Council of Nicaea reached many significant decisions which cannot be mentioned here. Its most significant decision, however, concerned the issue posed by Arius: Was the Son of a different essential nature than the Father? Arius, permitted to present his position first, boldly declared that he was. He was the Logos created "before all time," but, and here was the Arian by-word, "there was a time when he was not." This frank and forthright statement shocked many potential Arian sympathizers, for example, Eusebius of Caesarea. Eusebius, zealous as was Constantine to conserve the harmony of the Church and the Empire, suggested the adoption of a Palestinian creed, long thought to be that of his own church but now believed to have wider currency. Alexander and his youthful aid, Athanasius, rallied to this proposal with the proviso that the creed be changed so as to lock out Arius's chief themes. In its crucial revisions the new creed, signed by all except Arius and his ardent supporters, read that the Son was "of the same essence" (Greek *homoousios*) with us according to his humanity and "of the same essence" with the Father according to his divinity, that he existed "from all eternity," and that he was "begotten, not made." Those who refused to sign were anathematized and sent into exile.

Nicaea, unfortunately, by no means ended the Arian dispute. Within five years Arians, attacking particularly the Nicene term *homoousios* as unscriptural, garnered enough support virtually to overturn Nicaea between 330 and 361. Several things helped them: First of all, Constantine must have had many second thoughts about the decision, for, on his deathbed, he summoned the staunch Arian Eusebius of Nicomedia to administer baptism. Secondly, one of Constantine's sons, Constantius II, was an avowed Arian, intent upon making Arianism the faith of the Empire in the East, where he ruled. After the other son, Constans, died in 350, Arianism had a heyday for a decade. Constantius exiled proponents of Nicaea such as Athanasius and replaced them with Arians and introduced a reign of terror.

It is not surprising that Constantine's stepson, Julian, wanted to restore paganism. He embarrassed Christians by transplanting orthodox clergy to Arian churches and vice versa. He imitated Christian institutions, especially the Church's charities. Had he lived longer, he might have had greater success, but his untimely death in a Persian campaign ended his plan. Still, Christianity was now too well established to be totally supplanted, and the legendary words often put on his lips were a fitting epitaph for dying paganism, "You have conquered, O Galilean!"

After Julian Arianism thrived outside rather than inside the Empire, among the barbarians. Its success there was due especially to the brilliant missionary work of Ulfilas among the Goths. Much later mission effort by orthodox Christians, for

example, Ambrose, entailed the conversion of the Arian barbarians to Nicene orthodoxy. This process went on for a
couple of centuries as the barbarians moved southwards into
the western part of the Empire.

In the meantime two other heresies were developing. One,
called Macedonianism or, in Egypt, Photinianism, was a
later version of Arianism, but it entailed the subordination of
the Spirit rather than the subordination of the Son. The
other, called Apollinarianism after Apollinarius of Laodicea,
a friend and supporter of Athanasius, moved in exactly the
opposite direction from Arianism. Whereas Arius disputed
the Son's real divinity, Apollinarius queried his real humanity. Apollinarius recognized that the central problem in christology was why Jesus did not sin whereas all men do. Like
Athanasius, he said, because of the incarnation. However, he
went on to reason that, since sin is a result of human reason
going astray, Jesus must not have had a human mind. The
reason he did not sin, therefore, was because the divine
Logos or Son replaced his human mind.

Once more, the air in the East was filled with theological
shrapnel. Fortunately there was a triad of brilliant theolo-
gians who were equal to the task of resolving some of the
major concerns which had vexed the Church from Constantine on. These three, called the "great Cappadocians" — Basil
of Caesarea, Gregory of Nazianzus, and Gregory of Nyssa —
reinterpreted the western formula with an eye to meeting
eastern concern for *distinctness* of persons. The formula
which they proposed was that there is "one essence (*ousia*) in
three individualities (*hypostases*)." Compared with Tertullian's formula, this one came close to tri-theism and required
an insistence that the entire "essence" of divinity subsists in
each of the three "individualities" at the same time, such as
human nature subsists fully in three human beings at one
time or fire subsists in a torch, a furnace, and a candle flame
at one time. The mystery of the godhead lies in the fact
that the whole godhead subsists in each person at the same
time.

The Cappadocian formula was useful in the second universal council, meeting at Constantinople in 381. This Council
reiterated Nicaea, but it also condemned Macedonianism and
Apollinarianism.

The end of controversy was not in sight for the East, however. Arius and Apollinarius had just begun to raise the issue
of the relation between human and divine natures in the incarnation. With their emphasis upon divinity the Alexan-
drians tended to stress *unity* of natures. With their emphasis upon humanity the Antiochenes tended to stress the
distinctness of natures, or, better stated, the voluntariness of
interaction between human and divine. The fourth universal
council, meeting at Chalcedon in 451, favored the latter
view, though it also insisted upon more than a moral union
of the two natures which Nestorius, one-time Bishop of Constantinople taught. For the incarnate state the Son was one
person born of Mary, mother of God as well as mother of the
human nature of Jesus. But that carries the discussion beyond
the limits of time set for this book.

Monasticism

A myriad of important developments were taking place
between 200 and 400 which space will not allow the writer to
mention. He cannot conclude the story, however, without
considering the rise and development of monasticism, a phenomenon which was to have an immense bearing on Christianity's spread and survival during the next major phase of
its history.

In Christianity's earliest phase there were "eunuchs for the
kingdom's sake," but, as a self-concious movement, monasticism arose during the latter half of the third century as Christianity entered a period of peace and prosperity with the accession of Gallienus. Anthony of Egypt, who started his her-
mitage at age twenty, around the year 270, is regarded as its
"father," but other hermits preceded him.

The movement was a consequence of factors both external

and internal to Christianity. *Externally* it was motivated by a widespread dualistic world view which considered material things evil, by a desire for individual recognition in a state which tended to subordinate everything to its own ends, by the natural tendency of some persons to seek solitude, by historical factors such as the cessation of persecution which led to the influx of new converts and a deterioration of ecclesiastical discipline, and by the example of other movements both in the East and in the West. *Internally* it was prompted by Jesus' call for self-denial and cross-bearing, by the example of discipline inspired by many Christians in the primitive Church, by the example of the Jerusalem community in Acts 2 in sharing possessions, and by Paul's urging of celibacy in view of the expected end.

Early Christian monasticism took two forms. One was complete solitude and isolation from society as implied by the terms "monk" and "hermit." Very often, hermitic monasticism went to ridiculous extremes in fasting, prayer, and self-deprivation or mortification. The several types of hermits are revealing of the extremes. There were "dendrites," who lived in trees. There were "catenati," who loaded themselves down with chains. There were "stylites," who lived on pillars. A noted Syrian monk named Simeon lived more than thirty years atop a pillar in the desert of Syria laden with chains. He stood all night with his hands outstretched to heaven motionless or touched his forehead with his feet 1244 times in succession. An admiring biographer recorded that "kings and princes crouched at the foot of his pillar, hoping to catch, as if they were precious pearls, the vermin that dropped from his body." There were "apotactites" or "renunciators," who evidently approached deliberate suicide.

Hermitic monasticism took a heavy toll with its rigors. It is not surprising, therefore, that "cenobite" or "common life" monasticism developed soon afterwards. The first cenobite community, founded by a monk named Pachomius, involved hermits living in private cells in close proximity so that they could share the task of raising food, attend occasionally to a sick brother, and meet together for prayer and worship. Solitude was still the most prized element.

Monasticism spread rapidly in the third and fourth centuries. At about the time it originated in Egypt a more rigorous type may have developed in Syria. By the fourth century monastic communities thrived throughout the East — on Mount Sinai, in Palestine, in Asia Minor, as well as in Egypt and Syria. In 339 it was planted in the West when Athanasius brought Egyptian monks to Rome on one of his frequent exiles. From Rome it spread to Gaul, where Martin of Tours, a former Roman soldier, did much to plant it throughout the province.

Two "rules" helped to humanize and to bring monasticism closer within the circle of the institutional Church. One was drafted by Basil of Caesarea about 375 which had a powerful influence on eastern monasticism. The other was Cassian of Marseilles' *Institutes and Conferences* which he published after a lengthy stay in Egypt and which did much to shape western monasticism.

Monks, both men and women, played a signal role in the evangelization of the barbarian West during the fifth century and after. Although monasticism deteriorated for a century or so after Cassian, it was revivified and given new direction by Benedict of Nursia in 529. Above all, Benedict stabilized the life of monks by requiring them to reside in a single monastery for a lifetime except when founding new monastic communities.

Around A. D. 400

Little more can be added except a position statement concerning Christianity around A. D. 400. Numerically and legally it held an enviable place in both East and West. Paganism still survived, but it did so chiefly in the countryside and not in the cities. Strong emperors like Theodosius,

Gratian, and Honorius were moving to eliminate the last vestiges of Christianity's competitors. Victory was clearly at hand.

Not all things, however, were falling out in Christianity's favor. The East was shredded by theological controversies and divisions which would harden as time passed. People thronged the churches to hear great preachers such as John, later called "the golden mouth," but they brought with them many alien ideas and customs. By 400 Christianization had proceeded a long way, but it had required three quarters of a century of rigorous canonical disciplines devised by the bishops.

The West was entering a twilight period, soon to turn to night. The barbarians moved steadily southwards. In 410 the Vandals sacked Rome and crossed through Spain to North Africa. As Augustine lay dying in 430, they were beseiging the city of Hippo. The fear and trauma of the situation led to loss of nerve and moral collapse. Cities like Rome and Carthage became, as Salvian later described them, "sewers of indecency." The one institution which perhaps offered a glimmer of hope was the Church. But the Church, too, was to have its problems as the masses again laid the blame for the decay of the West at its feet. This was surely a "bum rap," but it took several centuries to prove that Christianity could also build a civilization.